Jennifer Davidson was born at the World's End, in Chelsea, London, in 1958. Educated primarily in the French Lycée system, she grew up in Egypt, Tunisia, Belgium, and Laos.

She attended King's College, Cambridge University, where she studied Philosophy before graduating in French, Russian, and Italian literature. In 1980, having moved to Berkeley, California, she worked in film and television production for two years.

After moving to Washington DC, she enjoyed a brief stint on Larry King's first live television show, followed by four years at the *National Geographic* Magazine, where she worked as a researcher and staff writer until leaving to devote herself full-time to writing fiction.

In 1993, she moved to Switzerland, where she lives with her husband and three children. Since 1990, she has been a commentator for National Public Radio's *All Things Considered.*

Jennifer Davidson

Stop Smelling My Rose!

with illustrations by Ann Arnold

Redgrove Press
Berkeley, California

Redgrove Press, P.O. Box 9075,
Berkeley, California, 94709

The author's royalties for this book will be
donated to support the AIDS work of the

in memory of her friend Paul
and to honor Diana, Princess of Wales.

Copyright
Text © 1997 by Jennifer Davidson
Illustrations © 1997 by Ann Arnold
All Rights Reserved

ISBN 0-9661092-0-1

Stop Smelling My Rose!

National Public Radio, NPR, and All Things Considered are registered service marks of National Public Radio, Inc.

For Nic, Dylan, Xanthe, and Lucy

with all my love

Contents

Acknowledgements	ix
Preface	xiii
Miss Redgrove	1
Humble Pie	5
First Admission	8
Good Morning! Channel 44!	11
Larry King, Mr. T., and Me	13
The Scorpion and the Hairbrush	18
Lady Mama	21
The Butler Never Smiles	27
Hamvillay	32
A Dizzying Selection of Parts	34
Bikers	37
Stop Smelling My Rose!	39
The Prophets of Doom	41
Contrary Old Lady	46
Medical Odyssey	48
Bert, Ernie, and Kierkegaard	53
Bear	55
Chasing Pimples	58

Thomas the Tank Engine	60
Home Again!	63
Intervention	65
My Friend Paul	68
Epiphany at Echo Lake	71
Parting	73
"Have a Nice Day!"	75
The Marmalade Lie	77
The Burglar and the Pink Shirt	79
Running with Rabbits	82
When in Rome...	84
The Lady and the Tree	86
Morning Blues	89
Disposal of Cadavers	91
Of Lice and Fleas	93
Egg Money	95
Free To Go	98
Flashbacks	100
From Guns to Bruises	103
Therapy & Quiche	106
A Piece of Advice	109
About the Artist	112

Acknowledgements

In my daydreams, I stand (tall and slim), illuminated by a spotlight, radiantly accepting an Oscar for something I have written. Then comes my favorite part, where I get to thank all the important people in my life.
On the off-chance this never comes true, I would like to take this opportunity to offer my own—heartfelt—thanks to:

Jane and Alan Davidson, for having me in the first place, and thereafter for loving and encouraging me;

My older sisters, Pamela and Caroline, for their love and loyalty, and for being less bossy as time goes by;

My grandmothers, Con and Lady Mama, whose wisdom and humor will never leave me;

My childhood teachers, Miss Banner and Miss Redgrove, who saw a spark in me and helped it ignite;

My friends De Fischler Herman and Ali Kahn, who persuaded me to submit my work to National Public Radio's *All Things Considered*;

Margaret Low Smith at NPR, who has patiently and expertly edited my work for radio;

Mario Fsadni, who suggested that I put together this

collection, and Val Fsadni, who held my hand when the going got tough;

Matilda Hartwell, Karen Ray, and Sarah Hamilton, for their helpful editorial advice, and for their friendship;

Sam Bloomfield, for his inspired editing, for all the delightful e-mails, and for giving me courage;

Ann Arnold and Ian Jackson, for the wine, the hot-water bottles, and the TLC when I stayed with them on my last trip to see my friend Paul;

My friend Paul, wherever he is, who made me laugh like no-one else, and Ann Webster, who I hope has by now met Paul somewhere out there in the ether;

Maggie Brodnick, Phil Hoby, Jane Buckland, Paul McCarroll, Maggie Graf, Tanya and Ueli Suter, Pat Wilson, Meli Walder, Nancy Graham Holm, Lorri Kerr-Atkinson, Elli Geiger, Marina Morari, Gail Charity, and Paul Sochaczewski and the Majorca Writing Workshop (Wendy! Tina! Monique!) for their unflagging encouragement;

My incredibly supportive agent and friend, Theresa Stefanidis (of the Stefanidis Agency, Inc. in Geneva), who is always a delight to work with;

My wonderful husband, Nic Spencer, who for the last eighteen years has been my best friend and chief supporter, and who, in the last six months, pulled all the stops out to help me on this book;

My son Dylan, who—at age ten—is one of my best literary advisers, and who uncomplainingly fixes lunch for himself and his sisters when his mother is writing;

My daughters Xanthe and Lucy, who delight me, and encourage me, and give me such joy;

and all my much-loved friends and relatives.

I would also like to thank some of my favorite writers for specific books that have provided me with distraction, solace, amusement, and wisdom—and helped me see the point of continuing to write:

Anne Tyler, especially for *Saint Maybe*
Frank Schaeffer, for *Portofino*
Alan Warner, for *Morvern Callar*
Vikram Seth, for *A Suitable Boy*
Anne Lamott, for *Bird by Bird*
Bill Bryson, for *Notes from a Small Island*
Sue Townsend, for all the *Adrian Mole* books
April Sinclair, for *Coffee Will Make You Black*
Helen Fielding, for *Bridget Jones's Diary*
Martha Manning, for *Undercurrents*
Penelope Lively, for *The Road to Lichfield*
Stephanie Grant, for *The Passion of Alice*
Lorrie Moore, for *Who Will Run the Frog Hospital*
Meera Syal, for *Anita and Me*

Preface

Some mothers, when asked what they would like their children to be when they grow up, will answer "oh, goodness, I don't mind. Whatever. Just so long as they are happy." My mother's answer, with regard to her three daughters, was rather more definite: "a Lawyer," she said, "a Doctor, or a Bridge Builder."

For better or for worse, she has ended up with a literary agent, a lecturer in Slavonic studies, and a writer.

I realize now that all my mother ever meant was that we should dare to fly high, that we could do any job we wished, and that our gender should in no way limit our choices.

I was a literal sort of child, however, and for a long time I thought I really ought to be a bridge builder.

Several years ago, I wrote a piece which aired on National Public Radio's *All Things Considered*, about my friend Paul, and his fear of admitting to his mother not only that he was gay, but also that he had AIDS. My editor at NPR called to say the piece was about to be broadcast, so I sat on the living-room floor and had the slightly strange experience of listening to my voice coming out of the radio, telling Paul's story.

Minutes later, the telephone rang, and a strange male voice said the words I had been waiting all my life to hear: "Is that Jennifer Davidson, the writer?" I gulped slightly, and said "I think so." He said he had been driving home when he heard my piece, and had pulled off the road and got my number from information. "I have a daughter," he said, then stopped short. "There's a conversation I should have had with her a long time ago, and I'm going to go home and talk to her now," he said. Before I could react, he said, "thank you," and hung up.

I realize now that I have in fact all along been trying to follow one of my mother's suggestions, if only metaphorically. Every day, when I sit down at my computer to write, I am, in my own way, doing my best to build bridges, albeit ones made only of words.

Jennifer Davidson
Switzerland, 1997

MISS REDGROVE

The first significant teacher in my life was called Miss Banner. Tall and elegant, she had beautiful fair hair swept up in a chignon, and never ever got ruffled. She wrote in a school report when I was seven years old "Jennifer will surely grow up to be a writer," a vote of confidence that cheers me to this day. It was certainly more encouraging than the depressingly well-deserved comment I received from a later teacher: "Jennifer: Learn Brevity!" she wrote, crushing me economically in just three words.

But the teacher I know I will never forget is Miss Redgrove. She walked into our classroom one sunny morning, some thirty years ago, exuding such extraordinary charisma that my schoolmates and I fell instantly silent and then, spontaneously, broke into slow and prolonged applause. This was an unheard of reception from us. We were a surprisingly unruly lot, given that we were supposed to be reasonably well-brought up, and were attending the not-inexpensive French Lycée in London. I don't know why we gave most teachers such short shrift and such a hard time. I remember one poor woman, Madame somebody, who was smallish and roundish, rather hen-like and not at all effectual, picking up a chair and hurling it at my friend Debby, who, it must be said, was behaving pretty impossibly at the time.

I can't begin to describe the elusive quality Miss Redgrove had that caused us to stop, instantly, by unspoken agreement, the squabbling, the giggling, the gossiping, the arm-wrestling, the pushing, the banging of books, the flicking of bits of blotting paper that we'd been merrily engaged in until she appeared in the doorway. I've never known anyone else have that effect.

She sat down at her desk, looked out at the sea of expectant faces, said "thank you" with a trace of a smile, and then got on with the business of turning English lessons into some of the most stimulating and mesmerizing hours any of us would ever know. She was extremely tall, more than six foot tall, and very thin. She had warm brown eyes and an incredible face: like Virginia Woolf, but less beautiful, with less symmetrical features. No: like Virginia Woolf, but *more* beautiful.

She sat down one day at her desk at the head of the classroom and—I can't imagine quite how—entirely missed the chair. She ended up sitting down, hard, on the plinth behind her desk. She was so tall that even in that position, her face and neck rose up above the desk. There was total silence in the classroom. You could have cut the air with a knife. Then she smiled and her smile grew and she started to laugh, and then finally, with a collective explosion of relief, we all laughed too, with her, until our stomachs ached and our eyes streamed.

She taught us Shakespeare and Dickens and Laurie Lee and e.e. cummings. She taught us lists of words that I remember to this day: moribund, vituperative, melancholic, acerbic, and asinine. She taught us to examine our concepts of honesty, astonishing me when she revealed that she would put a coin in a slot of a bathroom stall even if it were broken. She talked about sex to us, the only adult I ever knew as a child to come right out and say what a wonderful thing it was. She had a dreamy look in her eyes for a moment, then said briskly, "but you're much too young, of course, and you must wait." But now we knew sex was something worth waiting for (which was news for the girls, if not the boys). If Miss Redgrove said it was, it must be.

She managed to wring talent out of the dullest among us. Laconic, gum-chewing boys suddenly spat out their gum and started writing poems. Previously clothes- and gossip-obsessed girls arrived early to class, proudly bearing critiques of J.D.Salinger.

I remember vividly the day Miss Redgrove had us all push back our chairs and desks, and led an impromptu and very spirited drama workshop, until the head of the school, the dreaded Monsieur le Proviseur, stuck his nose in to see what the noise was all about. He gave her a meaningful glance and said he'd see her later, and there were no more drama workshops after that. (He was definitely asinine.)

Miss Redgrove, unbeknownst to us all, was not well. Always painfully thin, she grew dangerously so, and had to leave to be treated for long-term anorexia. I remember marching to the Proviseur's office, stamping my foot and demanding to know what had happened to her; for one day she was there and the next she wasn't and we were given no explanation. It was probably the first (though not the last) time in my life that I flatly refused to take no for an answer. Very reluctantly, Monsieur le Proviseur gave me the name of the hospital where she was, after making me swear not to tell anyone else. I found her there, and that day marked the beginning of a new phase, in which Miss Redgrove slowly metamorphosed from being my teacher into becoming Valerie Redgrove, my friend.

Valerie died some twenty years ago, at the age I am now. But Miss Redgrove, I know, lives on and will live forever, in the hearts and minds of anyone she ever taught.

HUMBLE PIE

My first attempts at job hunting in England might have been comical had they not, at the time, been so dispiriting. Freshly graduated from university, I approached, with equal enthusiasm and naivete, a large number of British newspapers, who, to my great surprise, were less than impressed with me.

"Can we see your clippings?" they demanded. "What newspapers or other publications have you written for?" I tried to look thoughtful before regretfully shaking my head. "Provincial papers?" I frowned. "Well, student publications, then?"

The more they probed, the worse it got. I considered mentioning "The Daisy Magazine," of which my sister Pamela published two issues, at around age nine, but on reflection realized that she had never actually allowed me to contribute anything.

I resorted to saying, slightly indignantly, "I've only just realized that I want to be a journalist!" Then it was their turn to shake their heads, after which they showed me the door. After a month or two of this, I concluded a change of venue was in order.

"The job prospects are much better in California," I said airily to friends in London when they questioned my impending move to Berkeley. "Remember, I'm American as well as British, so I can just as well job-hunt there." (The fact that my boyfriend had just recently moved there had nothing to do with it. Certainly not.)

And so, with at least a modicum of optimism, I set off for California. Berkeley, I kept telling myself firmly, was going to be a whole new kettle of fish. I would probably find a job there in no time flat.

I moved in with my boyfriend and promptly rearranged all the furniture (a lifelong hobby kindly tolerated by him both then and now). Then I set out once again to try and find someone willing to employ me.

After a few discouraging weeks, I joined a women's group, in the hopes that it might offer moral support. However, the other members were considerably older than I—dealing with divorces and errant teenagers while I agonized endlessly about job-hunting strategies: Should I a) try and get any old job? or b) hang on and wait for the ultimate position (whatever that might be)? I'll never forget one woman turning to me and saying "Jennifer, we have an expression in America that I think you should learn: It's 'Either Shit, or Get Off the Pot.'"

I decided, when I'd recovered, that this translated as an endorsement for plan a). So I gave up on breaking into journalism, and went off to register at a series of temping agencies in San Francisco.

The first interview went quite well until the young bearded interviewer read my answers to the "personality questionnaire." His eyes skimmed down the page until they reached question number 17, at which point he raised his eyebrows. The question was, "Do you consider yourself a humble person?"

I had given the matter about three seconds' thought, and had decided the right answer was obviously "no."

This is America, I reasoned, land of get-up-and-go. They must be trying to weed out unconfident, low-self-esteem, shrinking-violet types.

The interviewer (himself somewhat lacking in oomph, I couldn't help thinking) leaned towards me. "Not humble?" he said. I nodded confidently. He frowned, and gave a little cough. Then he dispensed a twenty-five minute lecture on the virtues of humility, and of the benefits of following the example offered us all by the good Lord Jesus Christ.

When the lecture finished, I mustered what was left of my fast-dwindling get-up-and-go and upped and went, thoroughly chastened, much humbled, and still jobless.

I alternated being exceedingly modest at ensuing interviews and projecting great self-confidence, never sure which approach would pay off. Something must have worked, because I did in the end find a job, stuffing envelopes for *Lovers of the Stinking Rose*, a garlic fan club with its own newsletter, the *Garlic Times*.

I couldn't decide what to write to my friends back in England, who had all by now found deeply impressive jobs in the civil service or at assorted publishing houses. Although I rather enjoyed stuffing envelopes, it wasn't quite the success story that I'd hoped to report back.

In the end, after some thought, I wrote "The weather is marvelous here. So is the food. Unfortunately, though, I am spending much of my time eating humble pie—which tastes much the same here as it did in England."

FIRST ADMISSION

I don't remember worrying much about how I would adjust to life in the U.S. after moving from England. I probably figured it would be a piece of cake—after all, I spoke the language, didn't I? I soon discovered I didn't.

Within hours of landing in the U.S. of A—in Berkeley, California, to be precise—I was disabused of my illusions. My boyfriend abandoned me briefly at a deli counter, saying airily "order yourself a sandwich," as he headed for the men's room.

I was still reading the menu, wondering what pastrami was and how you pronounced it, when the deli lady appeared. "I'd like a sandwich, please," I said nervously.

Now, in England, the term "sandwich" typically means two slices of limp white bread clamped around a single slice of meat or cheese. The sort of thing they serve on British Rail trains in triangular packets for rather too much money. "A ham sandwich," I added as an afterthought.

That's when it got complicated. "Smithfield, hickory-smoked, Westphalian?" said the deli lady all in one breath. I gulped. She barreled on. "Whole wheat, rye, pumpernickel, sourdough, Kaiser roll, French, white, sub, sunflower?"

I opened my mouth to say "I beg your pardon?" but she swept right on. "Lettuce, tomato, mayo, mustard, pickle, relish, hot peppers?" Then, rather mystifyingly, she added "sprouts?" "Brussels sprouts?" I thought, "in a sandwich?" Pencil poised over her pad, she continued: "Jack, Swiss, Provolone, Muenster?"

By now I was beginning to feel almost tearful. I mean all I wanted was a sandwich, for heaven's sakes, not the Spanish Inquisition. I pulled myself together. "Yes. Please," I said firmly. "Which?" said the woman

relentlessly. "Everything," I said with as much dignity as I could muster. I watched with horror as her pencil checked every box on her pad. She paused for a second. "White bread do you?" "Thank you," I whispered forlornly.

By the time my boyfriend reappeared from the men's room, he had a hard time finding me. I was half-hidden from view, slumped behind a mile-high sandwich that I felt too defeated to eat.

A couple of days later, when I'd more or less regained my confidence, I made the mistake of trying to find out, over the phone, how to get by bus from Berkeley to San Francisco.

Now, in England, streets and roads—much like people—are always respectfully addressed by their full titles. You would *never*, *ever*, refer to Oxford Street, for example, as just "Oxford," or say "meet me at Oxford and Regent at five."

And so when the kindly operator told me I should get off the bus at "First and Mission" this made no sense whatsoever to me.

"First admission to what?" I asked. "FIRST AND MISSION" said she, in a voice reserved for the foolishest of all possible fools. We spent a full five minutes in mutual frustration shouting first admission? and FIRST AND MISSION! to each other, before I finally hung up in despair.

After blowing my nose, I picked up the phone and called my boyfriend. "I've decided to go home," I said. "I don't like it here. I'm going back to England on the next plane."

And I would have done, too.

Only when push came to shove, I realized I didn't really want to go back—quite apart from which, I was far too intimidated at the prospect of calling for a cab to the airport.

GOOD MORNING! CHANNEL 44!

When I tired of stuffing envelopes for *Lovers of the Stinking Rose*, I decided to try and carve a niche for myself in Berkeley as a freelance editor. I was initially rather lethal, swiping with my red pen at any number of perfectly legitimate American words, (such as *envision* and *inquire*), because to my British-trained eye they looked all wrong. After my boyfriend kindly provided me with a Webster's dictionary, I became less trigger-happy, and settled down to edit an eclectic selection of books and manuscripts. I sailed fairly easily through a manual on motorcycle maintenance, but was grounded by an abstruse-to-the-point-of-unintelligibility tract on Sufism. I remember editing a cookbook, one of whose recipes opened with the words, "First, open a can of spaghetti."

Then I took on a job for a local bookseller, typing up his catalog of second-hand, botany-oriented books, which was restful, though not exactly exciting, work. (The high point of that job was discovering the existence of a book whose title—"The Potato and Its Wild Relatives"—still makes me smile to this day.)

Eventually, I got a job as a receptionist at a local TV station, where I learned to master the blinking switchboard buttons, and to trill "Good Morning! KBHK! Channel 44! Can I help you?" as instructed. The only thorn in my side was my predecessor, who filled in for me when I went to lunch. She used to unnerve me by spraying disinfectant and ostentatiously wiping down the desk and the chair where I had just been sitting. She was apparently critical of the way I placed things like the paper clips and the tape dispenser on my desk, and rearranged them every time she swished past in a cloud of perfume.

Just as the job was becoming humdrum, I was thrown a new challenge. KBHK specialized in airing old movies and reruns of programs like *Leave it to Beaver* and *Casper the Friendly Ghost*. Then, unfathomably, they acquired the rights to broadcast "The Deer Hunter"—a movie people had actually heard of! Naturally they were very keen to promote this new development. I was, therefore, instructed by the higher echelons to answer every incoming phone call to the station with "Good Morning! KBHK! Channel 44! Only seventeen more days till the Deer Hunter! Can I help you?" (The next day, the spiel changed to "Good Morning! KBHK! Channel 44! Only *sixteen* more days till the Deer Hunter!") I leave you to imagine the fury of callers repeatedly trying to reach a KBHK employee—forced to do so via the switchboard—and subjected each time to this tedious litany.

Occasionally, I tried injecting a note of irony to my voice, but people were generally too busy being incredulous or abusive to notice. I was positively giddy with relief the day I got to say "Only one more day till the Deer Hunter!"

After a while, I decided to move on. My only regret is that it didn't occur to me, the day I resigned, to answer the phone with "Good Morning! KBHK! Only fourteen more days till I'm outta here!"

LARRY KING, MR. T., AND ME

I was working in Berkeley as a film production assistant when my boyfriend announced that he wanted to accept a job offer from a company on the East Coast. "I don't think I'll go," I declared to Nancy, my boss and mentor at the time. She raised her eyebrows. "My Career," I explained. Nancy gave me a long hard look and said—quite accurately, as it turned out—"jobs are two a penny. Men as nice as Nic are extremely rare."

And so I arrived in Washington DC in 1983, young, unqualified, and determined to work in television. I relentlessly pestered the Executive Director of the newest show in town (Larry King's first venture into live TV) until he finally gave in and hired me. Armed with a crisp collection of business cards bearing an exalted title—Jennifer Davidson, Research Director, Larry King Show—I threw myself whole-heartedly into my first Proper Job.

One of my duties was to help generate ideas for guests on the show, and I brought to our daily meetings long lists of writers, actors, and artists that I particularly admired. "Let's get Laurence Olivier!" I would say, bursting with enthusiasm. "I bet if I could find a lead to him—" I would continue, faltering slightly as I was met with a set of politely blank faces.

Part of the problem was my British heritage, and a rather heavy-on-the-intellectual-side-of-things education. Mostly, however, I blame my parents. For some mysterious reason, they never believed in watching—

let alone owning—a television.

I therefore hold them entirely responsible for the yawning chasms in my knowledge of the world—and, more specifically, for the gaffes I kept making on the Larry King Show. "Who exactly *is* Lucille Ball?" I asked innocently on one memorable occasion. When I reported my colleagues' hilarity to my boyfriend (a fellow Brit, but one with normal, television-furnished parents), he looked at me goggle-eyed and said incredulously "You're joking. You can't possibly not know who Lucille Ball is!"

For a while I thought I might as well just go and jump into the Potomac. Instead, I learned to keep my mouth shut, and gradually absorbed, belatedly, a sort of rudimentary grasp of Who's Who in 20th-century entertainment. (To this day, however, I refuse to play Trivial Pursuit.)

The main part of my job—researching the guests, to provide fodder for Larry King's live, unedited, interviews—was less problematic. I spent countless happy hours digging up clippings from newspapers and magazines, occasionally even pre-interviewing someone famous.

I wrote a collection of—I thought—rather witty profiles of such disparate guests as Tip O'Neill, Frank Perdue, Roberta Flack, Robert Duvall, and Ralph Nader, not to mention various people who had seen UFOs or had undergone a sex change.

The only downside of all this hard work was that Larry King did not, as far as I know, ever actually read any of my carefully crafted profiles. He was at the time—perhaps still is—a firm believer in coming to his subjects fresh, untainted by preconceptions. I doggedly kept writing my pieces, for the edification of the other members of the staff, notably my friend Vallie, the show's eternally cheerful production assistant.

Finally, I made a pact with my producer and with Larry: I provided him with cards bearing a few trigger words—like "Roberta Flack: Cupcakes"—and he would, at least some of the time, use these for inspiration. (I was tempted to feed him entirely spurious leads: "Ask Zbigniew Brzezinski about cupcakes" would

have been good, for example, but I didn't, since I was determined to be the best Research Director ever.)

After a while, my producer, for reasons best known to herself, assigned me to Green Room duty: I was to play host to the show's guests as they waited to go on the air, hobnob, offer coffee and tea, and obtain their signatures on release forms. (It was, arguably, unwise to entrust these tasks to someone who was not only morbidly shy with strangers, but proven to be culturally impaired.)

I resolved to do my gung-ho best, even though anyone with half a brain could see that inimitably cheerful, get-along-with-anyone Vallie should have had the job. (When told to procure a live audience for the show, Vallie would head for the Smithsonian, where she would leap aboard parked tour buses full of Japanese tourists: "Spark up Your Tour!" she would cry, to rows of astonished Asian faces. "Come and see Larry King this Sunday! Live! Tickets are free!" To my eternal amazement—given that the show aired near midnight—she succeeded more often than not.)

Still, it was I, not Vallie, who faced the guests in the Green Room each Sunday evening, and I who had to find a way of breaking the ice with big, hulking, Mr. T., of A-Team fame. As I nervously hovered, offering coffee or tea, desperately trying to think of a topic of conversation, Mr. T. proceeded wordlessly (bar the occasional grunt) to undress in front of me, removing a pair of bright blue shorts from his shockingly muscular legs and substituting a pair of otherwise identical bright red ones. I, meanwhile, studiously checked my clipboard and the coffee machine. He then rifled at length in a large black bag, producing what must have been a couple of hundredweight of gold chains, which he spent a good quarter of an hour untangling and draping around his neck. After switching on his boom box, he cranked up the volume, and to the blaring sound of spiritual chanting, prostrated himself on the ground and started to pray.

Unsure of the protocol of the situation, half-wondering if I, too, should prostrate myself, I continued to lurk nearby with my clipboard and the release form. "Any minute now," I kept thinking, "the other guests will arrive," and I broke into a prickly sweat wondering how I was going to get them to mingle. (Expected that evening were Serge and Beate Klarsfeld, two serious and dedicated Nazi hunters, who had flown over from France to explain why they had devoted their lives to this cause.)

All good things tend to come to an end, and so, after six months, did the Larry King Show. After a while, I found a new job, at the *National Geographic* Magazine, where I acquired a new set of friends and colleagues. To celebrate, I threw a dinner-party. I devised a game in which everyone confided in me—ahead of time, and secretly—some fact about themselves that they had never before revealed. I then inscribed these, in question form, on a card.

After an appropriate amount of wine had been drunk, the guests were invited to match present company to cards bearing such arresting questions as "Who once crawled into an ice-making machine in a Holiday Inn, in order to win a bet?" "Who once mooned their sociology teacher?" "Who, aged five, used to ward off boredom by sewing her toes together?"

But the part that I liked best was the fact that *nobody* guessed the correct answer to the question "Who once spent the best part of a Sunday night with Mr. T. wearing only his underwear?"

THE SCORPION AND THE HAIRBRUSH

My father used to go to great lengths, when I was a child, to reassure me on the subject of burglars, of whom I was—like many children—inordinately afraid. Every night, after kissing me good night, he would climb up a small stepladder propped ready for the purpose, in order to check for absolutely certain that no miscreant was lurking on top of my cupboard.

We were living in Tunisia at the time, and my memories of going to sleep at night are filled with the sound of wild cats screaming at each other under the moon, and visions of venomous snakes slithering around the orange grove at the bottom of the garden.

(The snakes lived not only in the garden, but also in wooden crates in our garage, while my father researched and wrote a short treatise on Tunisian snakes and scorpions.)

I myself saw a few snakes, but never a scorpion, at least, not a live one. I did, however, spend many hours staring at a pickled specimen in a bottle. It used to lurch around rather unnervingly in its bath of formaldehyde, and I found it endlessly fascinating, particularly in view of its history.

This particular scorpion had, before being pickled, intruded rather spectacularly on a diplomatic party held one balmy evening in our garden. (I, being six years old at the time, had been banished to bed, thus missing all the fun, as usual.)

The scorpion had apparently emerged, with remarkably little fanfare, from under a bush, and sauntered down the paving stones, heading straight for the throng of guests, its poison-laden tail swinging, I imagine, idly from side to side. A guest promptly spotted it and screamed, and pandemonium ensued. Women in high heels and cocktail dresses (for we were in the mid 1960s) leaped onto the nearest tables (somewhat precarious, as I recall) and perched there, squawking, as my father, with considerable sang-froid, walked calmly down the path and captured the offending creature.

As I say, I wasn't there, but I can imagine the scene quite nicely, and in my mind it always ends with a big round of applause for my father, hero of the day.

You would think, if I had any sense, that I would have spent more time worrying about snakes and scorpions—which were a faint but real danger—rather than burglars, especially as we lived in a well-protected house with stout locks. But it was burglars who captured my childish imagination, and it was a burglar—not a snake or a scorpion—who invaded our house one night as my two sisters, my parents and I lay tranquilly sleeping in our various beds.

I don't know, as the burglar prowled on tiptoe through the darkened house, whether or not he came into my bedroom; my windows overlooked the garden, and what with the screaming of the cats and the slithering of the snakes, I doubt I'd have heard even the noisiest of intruders. At any rate, he managed to find my parents' room without much difficulty. He approached the bed on silent feet, reached under the mattress and had just retrieved my father's wallet—and was no doubt feeling quite pleased with himself—when my mother woke up.

She leaped instantly out of bed, and—pausing only to grab a weapon from her dressing-table—set off in hot pursuit. The burglar must have been startled, to say the least, at the sight of my pajama-clad mama hurtling down the corridor fiercely wielding a hairbrush. He was, in fact, sufficiently terrified to leap head-first through a glass door leading into the garden, leaving a jagged hole behind him, after which he fled off into the night, and, I am pleased to say, into the arms of the law. He reportedly told the police that he had never been so terrified in his entire life, and I can well believe it.

I felt very lucky, as a child, to have not just one heroic parent, but two. They stood, it seemed to me then, admirably poised and ready to defend me from any danger large or small. This, I believe, is how it should be. All children should enjoy the illusion, however fleeting, that their parents are invincible, and will keep them safe come hell or high water, come scorpions or burglars or tigers or spiders.

Sooner or later, of course, the scales drop. Recently, I regret to say, my parents were visited by another burglar. He managed to prowl quite thoroughly around all four floors of the house before being unmasked by a screaming houseguest.

My mother, lying peacefully next to my snoring father, slept entirely undisturbed through the break-in, her deceptively innocent-looking hairbrush untouched on her bedside table.

LADY MAMA

I was seven or eight years old when I first met Lady Mama, and I fell in love with her at once. She made wonderful little square toasted sandwiches in the oven, with assortedly strange fillings, and took me for sunny walks in Georgetown, so she could show me off to her friends, the local storekeepers. "Meet my granddaughter, from London," she would say, and they would smile at her pride in her plump, little, British-accented relative.

She herself was petite and elegant, and moved with the grace of the dancer she once was. She tried to get me to dance with her, in the living-room, cranking up old tunes on her gramophone, but I was far too shy, so she laughed, in the nicest possible way, and skipped off, with me in tow, in search of some other adventure more to my liking.

Rather to my mother's disapproval, Lady Mama used to hide a packet of Lifesavers under my pillow each night. My mother, who slept in an adjoining room, could hear the crunching as I lay in bed in the dark, and would give her mother lengthy lectures in the morning about rotting my teeth, but Lady Mama just laughed. I thought she was wonderful, and I followed her everywhere, happily looking for things that she had lost, notably her cigarettes and chocolates, to which she was particularly partial.

She sleepwalked, which I found a little alarming at first; but after the first few nights I got used to the spectre of Lady Mama in her nightdress, long grey hair flowing, passing through my room on her way round and round the house, all of whose rooms seemed to interconnect. I cried when I left, not knowing if or when I would see her again.

It was six years before I did, and I found, upon my return to Washington, DC, that we had both changed. I was now an adolescent, and she had developed Alzheimer's. "Tralalala and Tralalalee," she said, with a twinkle in her eye and the same spring in her step. She spoke a lot in poetry. "Well," she would say, thoughtfully, breaking a sometimes awkward silence as my mother and grandfather faced each other across the kitchen table, "I like Coffee, I like Tea, I Like the Boys," (pause, for the punch line) "and the Boys Like Me!"

I always laughed, no matter how often she said it. It was a good rhyme, and very well delivered, one of many in her repertoire: "Mabel Mabel, Sweet and Able" she would remark, eyeing me with mock severity, "*get your feet down off that table!*"

Then there was "Fourteen and seven...well that's not eleven?" which was a favorite, recited in a puzzled voice, as if she were a little disappointed by the misbehavior of numbers.

I found poems of hers scrawled on bits of paper tucked into drawers all around the house. "This is a beautiful, beautiful, house," she wrote once on the back of a ticket, "It can dance and sing on the telephone."

She heard music everywhere, and was electrified by the sound of a plane flying overhead. She would jump to her feet to conduct it, her arms rising in a triumphant crescendo as it passed above the roof, slowly falling again as it sped upon its way. She saw light and beauty wherever she went, except in the dark of night, when she was quiet and troubled.

When she was feeling sad, she would stare into the distance and say "Mary Lane has gone to Spain," again and again. Mary Lane was her daughter, an artist, who died of leukemia while away on a painting trip in Istanbul. Once, by way of an experiment, I said, quite gently, "Actually, Lady Mama, Mary Lane didn't go to Spain: she died." There was a pause, while my grandmother considered this, then she looked at me and in a flash of lucidity said, "That may be so, but I prefer to think that she went to Spain." As usual, she had the last word.

When morning broke, she loved to talk to the birds from the tiny balcony outside her window; she liked cardinals, she wrote, but had a special soft spot for the less fancy species: "Little sparrow chirping there, you're nondescript as my grey hair."

(Her long silvery hair was, in fact, far from nondescript, especially as she took to placing strange objects in it, weaving a silver fork, say, or even an oddly shaped bread crust, into a neat twist at the top of her head.)

It was in my grandmother's house that I first understood how very differently different people can see the same person: Where I was completely charmed by Lady Mama, my mother—her daughter—felt in turn responsible, worried, guilty, alarmed at the vagaries of her mind, and, no doubt, sad at the loss of the mother she had once known.

My grandfather, Robert, clearly felt burdened, physically and mentally worn down by the strain and responsibility of looking after his capricious and ever nimble wife.

Her attention flitted from thought to thought, much as she flitted from room to room, rearranging things, opening and closing windows, leaving notes. I found, in amongst the silverware in the kitchen, a note which read "Evelyn Crooks reads lots of books" (her maiden name was Crooks) and, in the drawer of her bedside table, a list of mundane items—tissues, milk, butter, orange juice—punctuated by "heavenly blue morning glories" all in capitals and with a big exclamation mark.

Under that was an old envelope, the back of which contained what I thought would make an unusual but touching epitaph: "I've lots of heart, but little head," it said. "I'll take a book and go to bed."

She charmed the many people who crossed her path, including total strangers. I watched her once, arm-in-arm with an incredibly handsome young man with flowing blond hair.

I went out to call her in for lunch. The handsome young man kept his eyes on her, gave me barely a look; "I'll be in in a minute," said Lady Mama. "when I've finished talking to my friend." "Well," I thought, in a slightly envious huff, "I like Coffee, I Like Tea, I like the Boys..."

Sadly, her habit of going out on little walks was, eventually, her downfall. One night, she left the house—accidentally left unlocked—and walked some fifteen blocks in the dark, enjoying, no doubt, the unusual tranquility of this, her neighborhood. At the intersection of 15th and P Street, she stepped off the curb; a passing car accidentally hit her, and she fell, fracturing her hip.

The phone rang jarringly, piercing the darkness at 4 a.m. An apologetic voice explained it was calling from the Admissions desk at Georgetown Hospital, and there was a "confused old lady" there with a broken hip and did we know anything about her?

It turned out that of all the rhymes Lady Mama could have come up with, the one she chose to repeat over and over again, as she lay on the stretcher under the fluorescent glare of hospital lights, was "I live at 3232 Prospect Avenue," which was not only quite right, but a good deal more helpful than, say, the one about fourteen and seven not making eleven.

(Later, they changed Prospect Avenue to Prospect Street, but by then my grandmother had long since died.)

As a child, I didn't really know what was wrong with Lady Mama; I don't suppose I thought anything was. Later, I found out that Alzheimer's disease was the explanation for her wandering mind, and that it was hereditary. Now, as medical research marches on, the disease shows signs of being preventable, curable, or at least containable.

I suppose, therefore, that I am no longer fated, as I once imagined, to follow in Lady Mama's footsteps. I guess I won't be talking in rhymes, conducting airplanes, or winding silverware into my hair.

The thought saddens me just a little. People speak of others having "lost" their mind, but I think perhaps you don't so much *lose* your mind as get lost in it.

Graceful, gentle, grey-haired Lady Mama taught me, unforgettably, when I was still young and impressionable, that there are worse places to be than lost in a mind full of songs and light, poetry and music, birds and boys.

THE BUTLER NEVER SMILES

As a seasoned diplomat's daughter, I learned early on to recognize the signs. As soon as my parents started holding hushed conversations behind closed doors and leaving stray atlases lying around the house, it could only mean one thing: Another overseas move was looming.

My sisters and I would speculate endlessly, and fruitlessly. We could rule out Holland, Egypt and Tunisia, where my father had already been posted, and England, where we now were, but that—needless to say—still left a fair number of possibilities. My father, meanwhile, led us to believe that he was bound by oath not to reveal the locale until it was absolutely official, and so we had to wait, bursting with impatience, until, with a single word—like "Brussels"—our fate was revealed.

I was fourteen when the last of these hushed conversations took place, and I pestered my father relentlessly, until he finally said "you won't even have heard of the place anyway, so what difference does it make?" This annoyed me no end, and when he finally, weeks later, said "Laos" I was thoroughly aggrieved. "I jolly well HAVE heard of it! It's next to Vietnam!" I shouted. "And Thailand!" I stormed off to slam my bedroom door, thus missing the news that my father was, for the first time in his career, to be made Ambassador.

My first view of Laos was from Thailand, across a

mile of brown and muddy water. Standing on the banks of the Mekong River, I watched a little boat chug-chugging its way over to pick up and deliver the New British Ambassador and his wife and daughters. All of us, not just my father, had climbed up a notch in the hierarchy. It was strange for me, a diplomat's daughter who had spent years quietly snickering at various ambassadors' children, to suddenly be in this role myself.

My mother—now promoted to Ambassador's Wife—had showed us a letter from her predecessor, describing The Residence—as the ambassador's house was grandly called—and revealing, to my slight dismay, that it came equipped with staff: a butler, an under-butler, a cook, a laundress, two gardeners and a driver.

The brief warned of the cook's various shortcomings, notably a propensity for interrupting, saying "yes, yes, I understand," and then going off and creating something entirely unexpected—a concoction of raw egg whites whipped up with sugar, for example, instead of meringues.

The letter continued with a eulogy of Chuan the butler, whose photograph was enclosed, and who was apparently impeccably professional, and ran the Residence like clockwork. There was, however, a caveat: "Be prepared for the fact that he always looks extremely gloomy," and, underlined twice, the sentence "*Worry*, if you see him smile. He never smiles except when disaster is looming."

At last, our very small boat arrived. We climbed in,

carefully, and sat back to enjoy the view. Roughly halfway across the Mekong, the boat's engine cut out. We started drifting—remarkably swiftly—downstream, and were just beginning to wonder where we'd end up if the engine couldn't be restarted, when several loud

explosions issued from shore. My parents exchanged looks; the boatman remained expressionless. I couldn't decide whether to panic, but since no-one else was, I, too, sat tight. At last, the engine fired up again. The rest of the twenty-minute crossing felt like an eternity.

When we finally disembarked, we found a welcome committee awaiting us at the river's muddy edge: several senior diplomats decked out in white uniforms, sporting strange hats, and looking distinctly flustered.

"There has been an attempted coup," said the Defence Attaché, tersely. "Some idiot once again trying to overthrow the government." He shook hands quickly with my father and continued. "You must proceed at once to the Residence; get underground if you can. Keep away from windows."

As we drove through the empty streets of Vientiane, we passed a massive, bizarre-looking concrete archway. The Defence Attaché explained that a visiting foreign dignitary had landed at Vientiane's somewhat ramshackle airport, been distressed by the state of the runway, and donated several thousands of tons of cement to resurface it.

The deeply grateful Lao, however, felt they couldn't possibly waste all this munificence on the airport, and so built a triumphal concrete arch instead—subsequently dubbed, the Defence Attaché noted dryly, "the vertical runway."

At last the driver pulled up in front of a palatial-looking house, and turned off the engine. The place was eerily quiet. As we climbed out, we were all simultaneously struck by a chilling sight. Emerging through the front door, clearly recognizable from his photograph, was Chuan the butler, impeccably dressed *and smiling*.

This was—for me at least—the first time I started to

take the business of the military coup really seriously. We trooped obediently inside and remained incarcerated for several hours, wondering whether we were about to be blown up, and if not, what lay ahead of us in this strange new land.

It was not until Chuan appeared, bearing drinks on a tray and wearing his normal funereal expression, that we knew the danger was over.

If memory serves me right, Chuan never smiled again in the course of the next three years, except once, on the occasion of the annual celebration of the Queen's Official Birthday.

The garden was bedecked with tables and chairs, the sun was shining, cut flowers were tastefully arranged in vases, cucumber sandwiches temptingly arrayed on trays, and my parents were standing ready to greet their guests.

Chuan, deftly effecting a few last-minute touches, looked reassuringly gloomy. He fractionally straightened a napkin, then glanced up at the sky. He stared for a second, and nodded slightly. Then he smiled.

Minutes later, when all the guests were gathered and the first speech was underway, a deafening crash of thunder rang out. Before anyone could move, the sky split open and unleashed the worst, most torrential, bone-drenching rainstorm you could ever imagine, utterly and irreparably flooding the festivities.

As people tripped and slipped and fell over each other in their mad dash for shelter, Chuan moved serenely through the chaos, a gentle half-smile playing upon his face.

HAMVILLAY

The road to the orphanage was long and hot, and studded along the way with grazing water buffalo. I felt nervous of what lay ahead, though I was in good company, a nice young man from UNICEF. He was twenty-three, and I sixteen, which was perhaps part of the allure of embarking on this long drive through the heat, to spend an afternoon playing with orphans.

The orphanage, which was off somewhere on the outskirts of Vientiane, was run by nuns, who were old and kind and full of smiles. I worried all the way there that the language barrier would get in the way, since I spoke no Laotian apart from please and thank you and numbers one to ten.

The children were cavorting around the compound, when we arrived, kicking up clouds of red dust as they played. My friend went off and left me to it, and I played in a not very effective way with the first group of children I bumped into. I was at an awkward age for this sort of thing: trying hard to be grown up, not at all sure that it suited me to run around and wave my arms and make a fool of myself as my older friend was doing with such enthusiasm and to such good effect. I was just beginning to feel a creeping sense of failure, and to wish I hadn't come, when help materialized, in the form of a very little girl called Hamvillay. She was curiously still; an oasis of calm among the wheeling, careening children. She looked old enough to be crawling, or even walking on her short, endearingly podgy little legs. But she sat, quite still, her eyes unmoving, unresponsive, disquietingly immobile.

Sensing for some reason that she was a kindred spirit—neither of us seemed quite to fit in, I suppose—I went and sat next to her and attempted to engage her attention. She did not react to my arrival, seeming neither pleased nor displeased. I said hello, and thank you, and counted to ten a few times, both forwards and backwards, but she remained entirely expressionless. I knew though, that she was there. She definitely was. She was somehow managing both to be there and not there at the same time.

I held her on my lap that day, and on many days in the ensuing months, with no discernible reaction on her part. I stayed with her because I was shy, and because I liked her, and because no-one else played with her. At first I thought I'd somehow break the barrier down, but soon I realized that wasn't to be.

The last time I went to the orphanage, a tiny miracle occurred. I had taken off a small gold ring I wore on my toe, and accidentally dropped it. As I reached to retrieve it, I saw Hamvillay's eyes move, fractionally but unmistakably, glancing down to where the ring lay in the dust. I picked it up and held it up in the sunlight. I moved it from hand to hand. Hamvillay's eyes followed it, again and again. I wanted to shout in triumph: "You *are* there! I knew you were!" But then I had to leave. I hugged her unmoving little body tight, and left.

Two weeks later, a friend wrote to say she'd visited the orphanage and that Hamvillay suddenly, out of the blue, had started to walk, to talk, and to smile.

A DIZZYING SELECTION OF PARTS

Until very recently if I so much as glanced at a set of assembly instructions, I'd start to sweat. Clumsy with nerves, I'd barely manage to wrestle open the little packets of knobs and screws and widgets, let alone connect them to the gizmos, doohickeys and whatnots portrayed in the instructions.

Eventually, in a thoroughly bad temper, I'd stomp off to find my husband, Nic. "Don't worry," he'd say, soothingly. "I'll take a look at it..." You can guess the rest, I'm sure: he glances briefly at the instructions and says, "look, this knob goes here, this widget there, just like in the picture." When I protest that the instructions are totally misleading, he says airily, "well, it's not very well drawn, I'll grant you that..." and goes back to whatever he was doing before.

Not long ago, I came across a book in which the author described feeling panic on encountering his first weaving loom and realizing he had no idea how it worked. Determined to figure it out by himself, he waved away all explanations, and simply stared at it and waited until, very slowly, it began to make sense.

"Aha!" I thought. "Something for me to try..." Not liking to do things by halves, I went out and bought a very complicated-looking roll-top desk. The box was stamped with the magic words "Assembly Required."

I read the instructions, and nearly fainted. Nic, peering over my shoulder, started to say "don't worry, it's not so bad..." but I shooed him out of the room, explaining that an Experiment was underway. I unpacked a dizzying selection of parts. I could feel my heart pounding as fear of failure gripped my nervous system and sent sweat shooting to my palms. But I persevered. Eventually, the floor was covered with pieces. "This will never work," I thought. Following the book's advice about relaxing, however, I sat on the floor in the lotus position, took a deep breath, and had another look at the instructions.

What an extraordinary set of hieroglyphics! Pieces marked A and B and C, all the way through to V! Baffling explanatory notes like "female cam lock" and "Flap Stay." There were numbered things, marked 3, 4, 7, and 10. While trying to find what had happened to 1, 2, 5 and 6, I discovered these were only the instructions for assembling the drawers! Hands trembling, I opened the 3-page drawing of my 7-drawer roll-top desk. And then I read the caveat "Design subject to change without notice."

"We have nothing to fear but fear itself," I said, nervously turning myself into two people so one could provide moral support to the other. Step one. "Lay the smaller of the two tops A on a hard, flat surface with the pre-routed grooves facing upward." Two tops A? I looked at the picture. I could only see one thing marked A. I subsided back into the lotus position. Every time I felt panic rising, I fought it back. "I will sit here all night," I said to myself, "if that's what it takes."

And indeed, it was growing dark outside. But as I stared at the pieces of wood and breathed deeply, they became, in some strange way, less threatening. And then, after a very long silence, it happened. Quietly, in the faintest of whispers, one of them spoke. "I'm piece A," it said. I stared hard, not moving a muscle. "Trust me," it said. "I'm piece A."

Reverently, I laid the smaller of two tops A on a hard flat surface with the prerouted grooves facing upward. And from then on, believe it or not, it was plain sailing.

Nowadays, when we buy something that needs assembly, I cheerfully hand it over to Nic. "Don't you want to do it?" he says.

"No thanks," I say airily. "It's too easy. You do it!"

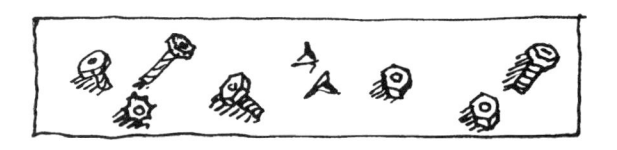

BIKERS

The sun was beginning to set, as my husband drove us back from a weekend away at North Carolina's Outer Banks. Staring out the window at cloud formations in the sky, I began to feel drowsy. I was distracted for a moment by two guys on big black and steel Harley Davidsons driving in tandem in front of us: I thought they looked rather like Tweedledum and Tweedledee, except that one was fat and the other thin. Soon, they disappeared into the distance. My head lolled and I was halfway into a dream when my husband hit the brake pedal and my eyes jerked open. Up ahead, inexplicably, the two motorcyclists lay splayed in the road, their crumpled bikes flung apart to the edges of the highway. There was no sign of what had caused the accident, and no-one else had stopped.

The thin man lay on the ground, slightly twisted, but apparently conscious. My husband went to him, and I walked over to where the one I'd thought of earlier as Tweedledum lay. He was a huge, hulking red-haired bear of a man with a big bushy beard and a black leather jacket and a beer gut spilling over the top of jeans. His arm, covered with a fuzz of red-gold hair, was heavily tattooed. He lay on his side, eyes closed, but breathing. The palm of his hand was cupped, facing the sky, and was filled with a welling pool of blood. He half-lifted his arm, trying to see what hurt, and I thought "he mustn't look, the blood will pour onto his face," so I said "hello," and his eyes sort of flickered in my direction and he held his hand still.

Then I panicked. Suddenly, I remembered who I was, and felt, in a rush, all the possible and possibly insurmountable differences between us: I, 23 years old, very English, a diplomat's daughter, and he, a huge, fortyish, rough-looking red-headed biker with tattoos.

I knew I had to get him talking to keep him conscious, but what in God's name was I going to say? I mentally started half a dozen sentences, only to kill them unspoken. Meanwhile, I was, in fact, speaking: "Don't worry," I said, "you'll be fine." Then I added, untruthfully, but hoping a passing motorist had called 911, "an ambulance is on its way. Don't worry. Everything's going to be all right." This, however, I knew, was not good enough. He had to speak, not me, to keep a grip on consciousness.

There are moments, I think, when guardian angels appear at our side and show us what to do—moments when we suddenly, miraculously, in some way transcend our ordinary selves. "Did you ever go fishing when you were a child?" I suddenly asked, out of the blue, I, who have never been fishing in my life.

And for twenty minutes, until the blessed sound of the ambulance's siren pealed through the air, the biker talked, haltingly, of going down to the river with his dad, of the swish of the line through the air, of long afternoons spent knee-deep in water, patiently waiting for a bite. He had been grimacing with pain, but for a moment there he smiled, fleetingly, even as the blood welled up and overflowed from his hand onto the highway.

STOP SMELLING MY ROSE!

My husband sat bolt upright in bed the other night and said—with a sort of passionate and accusatory fierceness—"STOP SMELLING MY ROSE!" I was sufficiently startled to be at a loss for words until I realized that in spite of his eyes being wide open, he was actually fast asleep. "You're talking rubbish, again," I said, with affection, as soon as I recognized the situation. "No I'm not," said he, somewhat belligerently, still asleep. We kept up a little volley of yes-you-ares and no-I'm-nots for a while, until either he woke up or I fell asleep, I'm not sure which.

I teased him a little the next morning, then forgot all about it, until by accident I happened upon a copy of *The Little Prince*, by Antoine de Saint Exupéry. Alone on the tiny planet he inhabits, the Little Prince lovingly tends a single rose, his only companion. He worries constantly about her welfare. He meets other roses on his travels, but they just don't compare. "You are beautiful, but you are empty" he says to them. "One could not die for you. To be sure, an ordinary passerby would think that my rose looked just like you. But she is more important than all the hundreds of you other roses: because it is she that I have watered; because it is for her that I have killed the caterpillars; because it is she that I have listened to, when she grumbled, or boasted, or even sometimes when she said nothing. Because she is my rose."

I think of my husband saying "Stop smelling my

rose!" And then I start to wonder. What if it is the spirit of the Little Prince speaking to me as my husband sleeps? Could he still be out there somewhere, valiantly defending his rose? If so, was he speaking to me? Or to someone else? And then I think, never mind the

little prince, maybe my husband has a rose? A rose that I don't know about? A rose that I was smelling, when perhaps I shouldn't have been? What if his sleep-talk is not rubbish after all?

Last night, my husband did it again. "The question is," he said, loudly piercing the darkness, "Will we make it across the swamp in time to get to the bathroom?"

Then he rolled over and slept soundly till morning, leaving me, wide awake, to ponder the question.

THE PROPHETS OF DOOM

An army of advice givers appeared out of nowhere soon after the announcement of my pregnancy. From the ranks of family, neighbors, single friends, married friends with children, friends without children, and the public at large, there emerged those whom I later dubbed The Prophets of Doom—all determined to set me straight with regard to pregnancy, childbirth, and the life ahead of me. This, I heard time after time, would never be the same again.

I had become pregnant very intentionally and very quickly. After taking pregnancy tests far too early to tell, I could hardly believe my eyes when the fifth magic bottle suddenly turned from pink to mauve (or was it mauve to pink?). I danced on air all the way to work. I made jokes to my husband about developing the official "pregnant glow," and lo and behold, I did.

"Morning sickness?" solicitous relatives and relative strangers soon asked enthusiastically. Feeling a bit of a fraud, I answered no, cautiously adding "at least not yet." Then came the inevitable response: "Just You Wait!" Soon, I was actively worrying about my lack of morning sickness. Helpful people pointed out that throwing up meant the body had high levels of the pregnancy hormone, which was a good thing. Did that then mean I was somehow not pregnant enough? When the second month had passed, I grew hopeful that I would get away with mere queasiness. "Just you wait," sang the Greek Chorus: "It hasn't kicked in yet."

It never did.

Initially, people were delighted at our news, just as I expected they would be. But what came hot on the heels of congratulations? The assumption that I must be feeling poorly. Expressions of sympathy. Sentences that began with "I must warn you about..." At the time, I put it down to pregnant paranoia, but in retrospect I am convinced that underlying the words of other parents was a certain gloating triumph. "Ha!" they seemed to say. "Welcome to The Club! Now you too will suffer!" I was told countless times that I could kiss good-bye to movies, reading books, cooking nice meals, and sex.

As my middle expanded during months four and five, I tried to tune out horror stories of runaway weight gain, flabby tummies, figures never regained, cavernous postpartum vaginas and so on. By the sixth month I was asking everyone "I do look pregnant, don't I? Not just fat?" Most people politely nodded yes. To distract myself, I whiled away untold hours drawing plans of how to turn the house upside down in order to accommodate the new baby.

Unbeknownst to me, during this idyllic time, the Prophets of Doom were busy behind the scenes. I was in for a shock from my well-meaning older sister. Over the course of a two-hour dinner, she waxed lyrical on the subject of postpartum depression, as I was likely to experience it. "I felt like throwing the baby out the window and then slitting my wrists" is the remark I remember most vividly, "and you will too." By the time dessert arrived, I was fighting a panic attack. My faint protest produced the hypothesis from my brother-in-law that since both my sisters had suffered from terrible postpartum depression, it was probably a genetic trait.

After that, I tried only to have conversations with supportive friends or with people who would keep off the subject altogether. No pregnancy talk. No childbirth talk. My ever-patient midwives were the saving

grace in all this, along with my parents-in-law, who came to visit for three weeks and managed to give me no advice whatsoever, for which I blessed them. Meanwhile, I learned to sidestep questions about what sort of birth I hoped to have. "You'll be screaming and pinching the nurses black and blue," said one childless friend. "God, the pain!" said another. "It's quite unimaginable. But don't worry, my labor lasted 45 hours and I survived."

Just as I was feeling safe, in the eighth-month home

stretch, a family member called to inquire if I'd yet experienced "those awful stabbing pains in your lower abdomen?" "No," said I, heart sinking. "Just You Wait!" said she, quick as a wink. Not having much choice in the matter, I waited. No pains. No swelling of the legs. No problems sleeping. No violent attacks of cramps. No wild, irrational mood swings.

When the big day finally dawned, I went to work, conscious of some slight cramping but blithely unaware of what it meant. After a morning meeting, I lunched with a friend who surreptitiously timed my winces and informed me that they were coming every six minutes.

I telephoned the midwife and was told this was labor. I called my husband, then returned to the meeting. Someone asked me if I needed to walk around, and I got to say "No, it's fine, I'm in labor but let's continue..." Differences at the meeting were suddenly ironed out at the speed of light. I took the Metro home, showered, and staggered out to the car, further along in my contractions than I'd realized. After about six hours at the hospital, I gave birth to Dylan James Spencer-Davidson, 8 lbs 1 oz.

I wonder, now, whether what I encountered is a widespread phenomenon. Perhaps I was simply unlucky in my pregnancy entourage. But I suspect that the cycle of life starting up anew stirs up powerful and ambivalent feelings, and that people unwittingly pass on their own ambivalence, couched in the robes of sage advice and greater experience. How I longed for positive stories with no caveats, for reassuring words, for optimistic predictions of how I would successfully cope with new demands.

Today, as a fully-fledged member of the Parental Club, I weigh my words carefully when talking to first-time pregnant mothers.

Here is the story I wish I'd heard when I was pregnant. It is all the better for being true.

> *Once upon a time, there was a woman who had an extremely healthy and happy pregnancy. She didn't have aches, and she didn't have pains; she didn't even throw up.*
>
> *Giving birth was hard but joyful work, and she drank champagne afterwards to toast her baby, her husband, her midwife, and the whole wide world.*
>
> *She stayed home for six happy months, then went back to work without trauma.*
>
> *She found an excellent babysitter who loved the baby, and whom the baby loved too.*
>
> *Her wonderful husband became an equally wonderful father, who shared the baby's care and all the household chores.*
>
> *They continued to cook nice meals, visit with their friends, talk about things other than babies, travel, go to movies and have sex—just as they did before the baby.*
>
> *And to this day, they are living happily ever after...(and with two more children, to boot.)*

CONTRARY OLD LADY

I plan to grow up one day to be a troublemaker. It may take a few years, but I've no doubt I'll get there in the end. I shall be a contrary old lady, prone to impossible opinions on all kinds of subjects, waving a cane around indignantly at the drop of a hat. Perhaps I'll follow in my grandmother's footsteps, and stride out into traffic with one hand imperiously upraised, as cars come screeching to a halt. Most importantly, though, I shall finally lay to rest the scourge of my youth: the whole tiresome business of Trying To Please Other People.

Swinging from a hammock in my dotage, I shall look back with amusement on my former self: Whatever happened to the little girl who used to rise at dawn to polish her mother's saucepans? I shall wonder. What happened to the child who ate a dried red chilli pepper merely because her sister suggested it might be an interesting experiment? Where is the young woman who said "is it OK if I push now? I know we're in the labor room, not the delivery room, but I really do need to push! If that's OK?" Ha! the little old lady will smirk. What a fool I was!

What joy to finally speak my mind, unfettered by the insecurity of youth! "No you can't cancel!" I will shriek down the phone at thoughtless dinner guests calling at the eleventh hour. "Certainly not. Or I shall never invite you again." "Go buy your own, I don't feel like lending it!" I shall snap at anyone who asks to borrow something. "Don't even think of hanging up without leaving a message!" my answering machine will announce, crossly.

The question is, though, how on earth to make the leap from here to there?

The other day a young child—old enough to know better—came up and wiped his nose on my bare leg. I wanted to leap up and shout "UGH! Don't EVER do that again, you horrible child!" But what did I do? I smiled feebly at the child's mother.

A few years ago, a woman I barely knew—I'd met her briefly in a prenatal class—asked me if I wouldn't mind looking after and breast-feeding her baby while she went on a vacation for a week to the Caribbean. I didn't say "no." I said "Oh, I'm afraid I'll be out of town that week." And then I actually heard myself say "I'm so sorry I can't help out!" Thinking of the contrary little old lady I hope to be, I hear a voice. "Idiot!" it says. "You can't let people get away with that sort of thing. You should have given her a piece of your mind!"

To which I reply—ever wanting to please—"You're right, of course. I'm so sorry!"

MEDICAL ODYSSEY

What started it all, I now realize, was my husband's deafening and practically incessant sneezing. A kind and sympathetic wife would doubtless have expressed concern, and proffered tissues. I, however, winced, shuddered, and said "Oh God, must you?" in a pained voice.

My husband's sneezing turned out to be a symptom of Mycoplasma Pneumonia, a flu-like disease which soon infected our son Dylan. When several antibiotics failed to work, Dylan's pediatrician decided I must be carrying and spreading the illness. He asked me to take a test with my doctor (five minutes, while you wait, he assured me) as soon as possible.

"It's Christmas Eve!" said my GP resentfully. "I can't see you today, I'm trying to get to the airport to meet my parents. Why on earth didn't you call before?" She offered an appointment in five days. I protested, since in the meantime Dylan would have to embark on yet more antibiotics. She referred me to the local hospital's Emergency Room.

Soon, a small menagerie consisting of myself, my sneezing husband, our houseguest Matilda, and little Dylan was facing a somewhat irritated Emergency Room physician. "A five-minute test for Mycoplasma?" he asked derisively. "Who told you that?" He took blood and told me to call back in five days. If the results were positive, the antibiotic of choice would be Erythromycin, which—he remarked casually—had a few side effects, including death. "But there's no reason to think you're allergic to it, is there?"

Although the results were inconclusive, I was put on a course of Erythromycin. Four days later, I developed a case of raging heartburn, followed by a fever and chills. The emergency room doctor who had prescribed the drug was no longer reachable; the staff there referred me back to my GP. She listened to my list of symptoms and I swear I heard her shrug her shoulders down the phone. "Stop taking the antibiotic, if it's upsetting your stomach," she said. I explained that I was under pediatrician's orders. Impatiently, she told me the choice was mine. I thanked her and hung up.

I spent that evening barking at my husband, who was doing his best to restrain me from exceeding the recommended dose of the antacid I'd bought. The next day, he drove me to see *his* doctor, who was duly impressed by the noises my stomach was making. He berated me for taking the antibiotics on an empty stomach (as per the pharmacist's instructions) and sent me on my way with strict instructions to stop taking the antibiotic, and with three new prescriptions in my pocket.

Some 12 hours later, at 3 a.m. to be precise, I started to itch. And when I say itch, I mean ITCH. Itching that cannot be conceived of by people who have not itched as I itched then. I woke up my husband. I complained. I tossed. I turned. I scratched. I told myself I was imagining it. I scratched some more. Finally, at dawn, I started calling pharmacists. "Itching?" they said thoughtfully. "Well, *lots* of drugs can cause itching."

I asked which of the four drugs I was taking was likely to be the culprit. But answers, there came none.

When in doubt, call your mother. Next, after rejecting her advice, call your friends. Then, if you itch badly enough, try everything that anyone—mother included—has suggested. Calamine lotion; baby powder; ginseng. Herbal tea; warm baths, cold baths, no baths. A teaspoon of cyanide in warm milk? Sure, why not? The only thing that worked was scratching.

During the next six weeks, I turned this into something of an art form. My feet bled from nocturnal clawing. I cut my nails short but, when the urge seized me, even my blunt little nails could carve terrifying demonic weals. My husband moved out of the bedroom. Then I developed a rash on my chest.

"I think you have what we call 'chemical' hepatitis," said the allergist. "Probably from taking the Erythromycin. The itching will diminish as the liver recovers," he added, "but not for several weeks. Possibly months." I reeled. "As to the rash," he added, "I'd like a dermatologist to take a look at that."

I was surprised to find, on the dermatologist's insurance form, a box for patients' nicknames; I wrote NONE firmly. He consulted my form breezily and said "Hi, Jenny. What can we do for you today?" He then summarily interrupted my explanation, ushered me into a large examining room with enormous windows overlooking a parking lot, and disappeared.

There were no drapes or blinds. I removed my glasses, and figured that if I couldn't see them, the hordes of Peeping Toms below couldn't see me either.

Then I unveiled my top half and climbed onto a sort of raised throne in the middle of the room, and waited.

"Well, Jenny," he said. "I don't know exactly what this is. Probably nothing. But I suggest we do a biopsy, just to make sure." He was applying alcohol to my chest as he spoke and marking a little red circle on my chest with some sort of crayon. Then he loaded a syringe.

"What does a biopsy entail?" I asked. Then I felt the needle pierce my skin and he began drilling into me with some sort of ghastly machine that emitted acrid fumes of burning flesh.

"Feeling dizzy, Jenny?" He reclined the chair abruptly so that my head was nearly touching the floor and broke an acrid pellet of something under my nose. The sickening smell mingled with the fumes of burning flesh, and I felt as though I'd tumbled into some ghastly upside-down nightmare, in which a doctor who kept calling me Jenny was doing horrible things to me. Then he swung the chair upright again with breathtaking speed, and I was still in the nightmare, but at least now the right way up.

Later, when the scar from the biopsy became infected, I consulted another dermatologist. "Scarring is not unusual," he said. "That's why we don't do biopsies unless we're sure they're absolutely necessary. What was the result, by the way?" "Normal," I said. "I see," said he, with slightly raised eyebrows. "Well," he concluded, "I can do something to relieve the swelling and the itching, but it will take a series of injections over the next year before the scar is completely flattened."

And now, exactly a year later, as the scar has more or less receded, my husband has developed a ghastly, hacking cough that has set the house a-shaking on its foundations and shoots my nerves to hell and back at unexpected moments.

Our son is sick, too, and the other day, we took him to see our pediatrician. He said he hoped we all had Mycoplasma, not just some random virus, so that we could be treated promptly with Erythromycin. I gasped slightly, thanked him, and left.

At least one good thing has come out of all this, however, at least as far as Nic is concerned. Now, when he is sick, I humbly minister to his every need. I produce tissues, and cough drops, hot chicken soup, and steaming drinks of hot lemon and honey.

A wiser, kinder, gentler wife am I.

BERT, ERNIE, AND KIERKEGAARD

I used to wonder how I would change when I became a parent. The one thing that never occurred to me was that I—the quintessential Not-A-Morning-Person, I who could barely be civil before breakfast to my own husband—would ever be converted to the early hours. And yet, at least for the moment, this has come to pass. Groggy and grumpy as I arise at 7.00, I tune in to the family of zany monsters who cavort so bewitchingly each morning on television's Sesame Street. How refreshing to meet someone even worse-tempered than myself in the form of Oscar the Grouch! How soothing to listen to the Count methodically counting his bats, as my two-and-a-half-year-old son resists getting dressed. (My sometimes-serious husband has been infected too; I swear I heard him singing "Batty batty batty batty batty batty bat" the other day, as he set off for work.)

"I want toast," says my son plaintively. "Just a minute, Mummy's busy," I reply. Entranced, I watch a reflection of my own marriage unfold, as Bert and Ernie quibble into the wee hours. And I wonder: are there other Lady-Ernies out there, wide awake by the light of the moon, wanting to talk, while their taciturn Bert-husbands wearily pull pillows over their heads? Is this show really just for children?

The Sesame Street creatures are funny and endearing, and sometimes even wise. Take Ernie's excitement when he realizes—thanks to kindly intervention by Hoots the Owl—that he *can* play the saxophone after all. He just needs to free up his hands first, by putting down his beloved rubber ducky. I always knew there was a way to have one's cake and eat it too !

When I was a teenager, my father took me aside and said he wanted to share with me a very important piece of philosophy. This was contained, he said ponderously, in just two words. Two words by Kierkegaard. I waited with bated breath. "Either, Or," he said. I was less than impressed. When pushed for a translation, my father said, "well, basically what I'm saying is, either you waste time playing with your friends and fail all your exams, or you study hard and succeed."

Nowadays, I instinctively reject black and white advice. Either you work or you play? Either you have a career or you have children? Certainly not! Sometime I must call my father and tell him to forget Kierkegaard and his wretched "Either/Or." Life, I now know, thanks to Ernie, is a balancing act.

You just need to know when to put down the ducky.

BEAR

I was rather scornful, as a child, of children who had dolls. It seemed obvious to me that a bear was the thing to have, one full of character, in the proud tradition of Winnie the Pooh and Paddington. My own bear was a fine member of the species: his nose permanently squashed from travelling in suitcases, his left ear ragged from being rubbed as I fell asleep.

Bear led a nomadic life, moving between continents according to the whims of the British Diplomatic Service, which periodically relocated my father and his family. He almost got left behind once, when we moved from Egypt back to London. After a certain amount of delicate negotiating, he was allowed to travel home in the embassy's diplomatic pouch, disguised as a highly important document.

For most of my childhood, I was convinced Bear was alive. This idea was planted by my older sister Pamela, who had great fun with it. "Bear talks to ME!" she would say. "No he doesn't!" I'd say, dreadfully upset. "Oh yes he does," she would counter. "He says he may talk to you one day. When you're older. But then again, he may not."

I used to spend hours late at night pleading with Bear. "I know you're alive," I'd say. "Please speak to me! Just one word. Any word. Please." And I'd stare at him intently in the dark.

Bear would stare back, his black button eyes unwavering. Night after night, I fell asleep disappointed.

"Let's leave the living-room," said my sister, firmly elbowing me out the door ahead of her, "and see if Bear moves while we're gone." While my back was turned, I later realized, she must have given Bear a quick kick. Outside, I waited anxiously. "There!" said Pamela triumphantly flinging open the door. And sure enough, there was Bear, on the far side of the room.

I redoubled my efforts. "Please Bear," I whispered by the light of the moon. "Please talk to me. Why do you talk to Pamela when you're MY bear?" Silence. Sometimes I grew so frustrated that poor Bear got shouted at or put in the corner, though later I was always terribly repentant.

Bear was such a feature of my life that I decided, when I was ten, that I could never get married. How could I possibly give up Bear—my loyal playmate, confidant, friend, and sleep-mate—for a mere husband? In fact, giving him up at all was a major disincentive to the whole business of growing up, until I discovered that a friend of my sister's still had her bear, and she was twenty-two!

So Bear and I stayed together. At college, Bear was introduced to each of my boyfriends in turn, and when I decided to follow one of them to the States, Bear sighed a silent little sigh, and submitted once more to being stuffed nose-down in a suitcase.

Later, when we were married, Bear honeymooned with us on a Greek island, and several years after that, he attended the birth of our first child, providing moral support from the depths of a grey canvas bag.

Today, Bear sits regally on top of a cupboard in our

bedroom—next to my husband's bear, actually. I thought I'd made peace long ago with the idea that Bear might never speak to me. But then the other day, my son asked to play with him. "No," I said. "He's a very *old* bear. He's tired, and he doesn't want to be disturbed. He just likes to sit there quietly."

"No he doesn't" said my son. "He wants to play with me. He told me so."

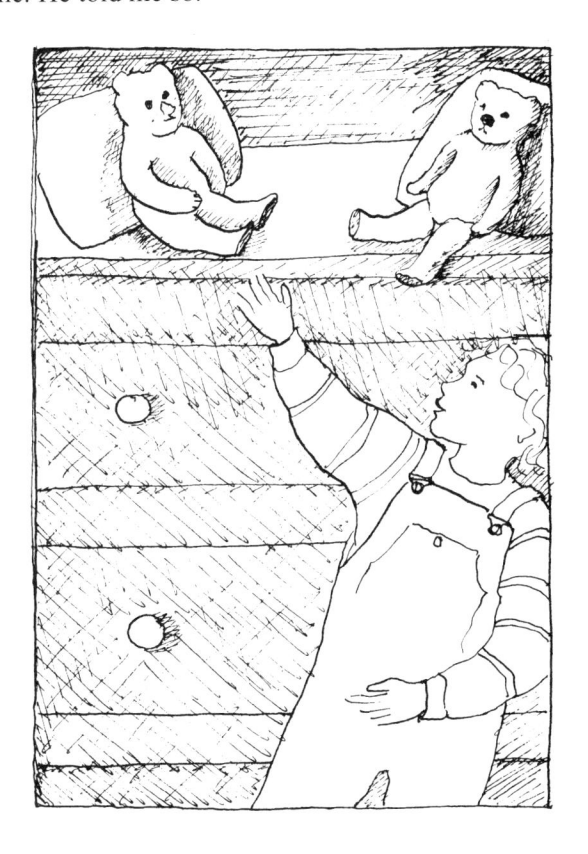

CHASING PIMPLES

My sister Pamela once produced what I now realize was an important philosophical insight, while standing in front of a mirror applying yet another magic potion to her blemished adolescent complexion. "It's all an illusion," she said with sudden passion. "You think you're getting rid of a pimple, but actually, all that's happening is that you're endlessly chasing it round and round your face." And with that, she snapped the lid back on the potion and left the room. At the time, I must admit, I wasn't particularly struck. Being four years younger, I was smugly content with my complexion.

But nowadays I often think of her remark. Here I am, constantly striving toward some mythical perfect day when I'll finish writing my play, have a tidy house, cheerful children, money in the bank, supper on the table, and—if possible—thin legs. Needless to say, it never happens. But the funny thing is that anytime I get even close to this idyllic state—let's say when I've dealt with everything except the play, the money and the legs—some new worry always materializes out of thin air. Like the air conditioner breaks. Or the car. Or the car and the air conditioner. And suddenly, I'm spending all day on the phone discussing carburetors and compressors. "Oh well... As soon as this is dealt with," I think, ever the optimist, "I'll get back to working on the Grand Plan." But somehow it never works out that way.

One of the things that gets in the way is being a

parent. I've decided parenting is pretty much like chasing a pimple round your face too. I used to think it was something you could learn, get good at, and then just keep on doing—like riding a bike, maybe. But as soon as my husband and I get vaguely on top of one issue—how to get our four-year-old to eat a green vegetable, for example, then our baby daughter produces some new behavior—continuous raucous screaming springs to mind—that has us scratching our heads again and heading back to the drawing board. And so it goes, on and on—an endless circular dance of parental authority versus child's ingenuity, the acne lotion versus the pimple...

Meanwhile, of course, the house is a mess, my play is frozen in time, supper is only in the back of our minds, money is almost nonexistent and my legs don't bear thinking about.

Still, there is at least one way that I'm ahead of the game. In ten years or so, when my son hits adolescence, I shall be ready with a piece of advice that should save him countless hours of anguish. "Don't even try to get rid of them," I shall say, as he peers disconsolately into the mirror. "They're nothing but a philosophical concept."

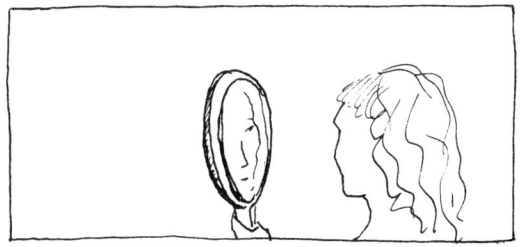

THOMAS THE TANK ENGINE

The first sign I had that we were at war* was when I arrived at London's Heathrow airport to find the place full of soldiers with machine guns. I'd spent the previous week at my father's hospital bedside in London, as he recovered from a heart attack. Now I was attempting to fly home to my husband and children in Washington, DC.

I check in obediently three hours before take-off. Solemnly, I answer questions about my luggage. Yes, I packed it myself. Yes, there is one electrical item. Sheepishly, I describe a device for pulling hairs out of one's legs. No, no weapons. Then I go hunting for last-minute gifts: a book called Mr. Grumpy and a Thomas the Tank Engine for my son, some Stilton for my husband, and a biography of Sylvia Plath for myself.

At last it's time to board Pan Am flight 107. As we taxi down the runway, I start the preface to the Sylvia Plath book. Then the plane stops. There is a mechanical problem, with one of the radios. An hour later, though, we take off. Foolishly, we applaud.

Just as I'm getting engrossed in Sylvia Plath's childhood, the captain announces another mechanical problem: The plane will have to turn round and fly back to London. Hours later, back where we started, I deplane, lugging my coat, Stilton, Thomas the Tank Engine and Mr. Grumpy behind me. Soon we are on a new flight, Pan Am 11, this time bound for New York, not Washington, but let's not be picky. I read about

---

* the Gulf War

Sylvia Plath leaving for college as the plane taxies down the runway. Nobody bothers to cheer this time, which is just as well, as a few seconds later the plane stops, and the captain announces a mechanical problem. It's the hydraulics, this time. Unfortunately, they can't seem to fix it. And so, Sylvia Plath, Mr. Grumpy, Thomas the Tank Engine and I check in dispiritedly to the Sheraton Heathrow Hotel, along with some 400 other passengers.

Bright and early, at 6:45 the next morning, I am back at Terminal Three, explaining all over again about the device for pulling hair out of one's legs. Then I revisit the Stilton store and buy two salamis, some back bacon, a pot of lemon curd, a packet of Twiglets and a bar of chocolate.

Aboard Pan Am flight 11 for the second time, I look for my place in the Sylvia Plath book. At this point, a young Englishman leans over and says "You were on that flight yesterday that turned back, weren't you?" And he adds, with relish. "It wasn't a mechanical problem. That plane was under threat: that's why it came back. The American Embassy in London got a tip-off." I thank him for the information, and read about Sylvia Plath's first suicide attempt as the plane taxies down the runway. Then the plane stops. The captain apologizes. New security measures are in effect, and we must return to the gate, deplane, and identify our luggage.

Along with Thomas, Mr. Grumpy, Sylvia Plath, the Stilton, salamis, back bacon, lemon curd, Twiglets, and chocolate, I deplane again. I call my husband and fight back tears as I tell him I have now been on two flights under threat of terrorist attack. I make sure to say "I love you," in case these are my last words. Out on the tarmac, I identify my bag. Its bright yellow luggage label is weeping black ink under the pouring rain. I board the plane again and wonder what my mother will do if my plane blows up. Will she tell my father? Will he see it on the hospital TV?

I spend most of the ensuing flight thinking things like "of course, when a plane does blow up, you don't have any warning, you're just sitting there, like I am, staring out the window..." Then I read Sylvia Plath as if my life depends on it.

Nine hours later, alive and fortified by a stiff drink, I board Pan Am Flight 6011R from New York to Washington DC and prepare, for the fifth and last time in 30 hours, for take-off. And take-off we do. Through a still and starry night we fly, as if guided by guardian angels, back to our husbands, our wives, our children, our friends.

And now, the salamis and Stilton are long-since eaten, and my father is home from the hospital. I've finished the Plath biography, and my son has lost the Mr. Grumpy book. But at least Thomas the Tank Engine sits safely on his bedstead, a sturdy little survivor, a silent reminder of my journey, and of the distant war that daily reaches out to touch everyone, everywhere, in some way.

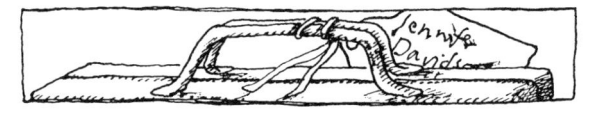

HOME AGAIN!

I paid a visit recently to my homeland—merrie old England, hallowed land of Shakespeare, country pubs and biscuits for tea. I felt thoroughly sentimental as we landed in a cold drizzle. "Home again," I thought. "At last."

One or two things had changed since my last visit: a fish and chip shop, I noticed with a sort of fascinated horror, listed "Burger in Batter, 99P" right after cod and haddock... But on the whole, England seemed comfortingly familiar. Until in the middle of one night my husband groaned, clutched his stomach, and demanded to go to the hospital.

Now in the States, I'm a veteran at this sort of thing. Hop in the car, or grab a cab and within minutes you're in a bustling high-tech emergency room. But here, I wasn't quite sure what to do next. I called the hospital. "I know I sound English" I said, rather pathetically, "but actually I live in America and I'm not sure any more how things work here... Can I bring my husband straight to the emergency room?" "Oh no, dear," said whoever I spoke to, "not without being referred by your GP."

And so, at 2:30 a.m., a freshly-shaved and remarkably cheerful young doctor arrived on our doorstep. He prodded my husband's stomach. Nic screamed. The doctor tugged his chin. Then he called the hospital. The hospital sent an ambulance.

We pulled up at the back of a dark building that

looked disturbingly like a deserted warehouse. "Here we are, love" said the ambulance driver, "Just ring the bell." So I did. "Ding dong!" went the doorbell. After a few minutes a light came on. "Hello," said a nurse—who was carrying a cup of tea—as she unlocked the door. She parked my husband's stretcher in a small cubicle. "You wait here while I go and look for the doctor." An hour passed before a resident appeared, diagnosed a kidney stone, and disappeared again. Another hour passed before my husband—who was now screaming in pain—received a painkiller.

At dawn he was admitted to a huge, Dickensian ward of elderly gentlemen. By late afternoon, he was feeling fine but hadn't seen a doctor, and wasn't being discharged. I was at a loss to know what to do. "Can we leave?" I asked finally. "Oh no," said the nurse. "Not till the X-rays come down." "Oh," I said, and meekly went away again.

An hour and a half later I enquired politely where the X-rays had to come down from. "Upstairs" said the nurse. "Well, can I go and fetch them?" I asked, feeling a growing sense of American outrage at the sheer inefficiency of it all. "Tell you what," said the nurse, "I'll pop up and get them myself." And so we were finally free. The very next day, we raced to the airport.

I felt an enormous sense of relief as our plane took off. Finally, we were on our way, back to the land of bustling emergency rooms and bright lights, where fast-moving people drink coffee instead of tea. I peered out the window as we landed.

"Home again," I said to myself. "At last."

INTERVENTION

I sat on a metro train in Washington DC, a few years ago, riding home from my job downtown. As usual, I was keeping to myself—eyes glued to my book, trying to tune out the crush of people—when out of the corner of my eye I caught sight of a little boy, about three, standing next to a woman.

He was determinedly pulling on one end of her scarf. I assumed she was his mother, but was puzzled when she ignored him. I thought perhaps she hadn't noticed. The little boy's tugs were growing more insistent. The woman kept staring straight ahead. The boy began to cry.

The other passengers began to look uncomfortable. "Mama" cried the boy, looking up at the frozen figure above him, "mama!" The woman stood there, impervious. "She must have had a bad day," I thought. "Or maybe he just did something dreadful, and she's furious at him. She'll relent in a minute, surely."

By now the boy was desperate, tugging harder and harder at the scarf. "Talk to him," I willed the mother, "say something, anything." I tried to catch the boy's eye, but he was single-mindedly focused, now crying loudly, tugging, tugging at the scarf that was his only link to his mother. His distress was catching. I wanted to do something, but I couldn't for the life of me think what. Then we arrived at my station, and automatically I got out of the train. I went over and over the scene as I walked home, wondering what, if anything, I could have done.

This summer, history repeated itself, and I faced another dilemma. This time, though, words—not silence—were the weapon being used.

I was getting dressed after a wonderful swim in a lake in Maine, when I heard a woman in the cubicle adjoining mine: "Bend over RIGHT NOW and put your hands on the ground," she said. I stiffened, wondering what was going on. "Please, Mommy, let me," said a child tearfully. "Bend over right now, Jackie. You are filthy! Now bend over!"

The woman's voice was quivering with anger. "Please let me do it, Mommy," said the girl, who was now sobbing. She sounded very young; when I caught a glimpse of her later, I saw she was in fact about nine or ten.

By now I was fully dressed in my cubicle, clasping my wet towel, mesmerized. "Jackie, bend over right now or I am going to push you over" said the woman, her voice snapping. I remember thinking, through a sort of fog, "my God, this is abuse, less than a foot away from where I stand."

I stepped out of my cubicle. The mother spoke again. "Jackie," she said through gritted teeth, "I don't want to hurt you, don't *make me* hurt you—" I stood rooted to the spot, the whole world tuned out: just the wooden door, open at top and bottom, the woman behind it, and the child crying.

At first I'd wanted to shout angrily, "you shouldn't talk to anyone like that. You shouldn't even talk to a dog like that!" but in the end that's not what came out of my mouth.

With no idea of what I was about to say or do, I leaned over, so my mouth was right next to the door, and I spoke. Very softly, I said, "If you need help, I'm right here and I can take over. I know what it's like to be angry at your child, I really do. If you need a minute to catch your breath, I can take over."

There was total silence. "I really do understand," I said. And the strange thing was, I did. Finally the woman spoke. "It's okay, we're fine," she said. Her voice was flat, drained of anger. "If you're sure..." I said, hovering. Then I left, shaking.

I went back to the beach, scooped up my two-year-old daughter, and hugged her tight. I spent a long time later wondering whether my intervention had been right, whether I might actually have made things worse for Jackie. To this day, I still don't know the answer.

MY FRIEND PAUL

I sat on the plane from Washington DC to San Francisco in a strange kind of limbo, alternately reliving one phone conversation and rehearsing another. My friend Paul had sounded quite cheerful as he explained why he was in the hospital. He said he'd picked up a virus on a recent vacation in Europe, and I almost believed him, but in the end, on a hunch, I said "Paul, this isn't AIDS-related, is it?" and then there was a pause that seemed to last forever, which he broke, finally, with a single "yes" that swept away years of deception and covering up and in-the-closethood.

We talked for a long time. He was tormented about whether—or how—to tell his mother, widowed a few years ago, alone in a small town in Wales; I said I was sure she would want to know, and I offered to make the call. He seemed relieved. The next day, without telling him, I caught a plane to San Francisco. I spent much of the flight practising what to say: "Hello, I don't know if you remember me, but this is Paul's friend Jennifer, in America," only I couldn't seem to get any further.

After Paul got over the shock of me appearing unexpectedly at his bedside, we talked more about his mother. He wanted her to know, but was afraid she wouldn't be able to cope. "She's all on her own, she'll get hysterical," he said, just as I was finally setting off for a pay phone with his blessing. I paused. I wavered. Then I had a saving thought. "If she gets hysterical, that's okay, it's her way of dealing with things," I said.

"I'll stay on the phone until she's all right. I promise. I'll stay on all night if necessary."

So, finally, he lay back, and with the look of a condemned prisoner awaiting the guillotine, he let me go. The phone rang and rang, and I thought "I don't believe it, she's out!" and then a cheerful voice answered, and I said "hello, I don't know if you remember me, but this is Paul's friend Jennifer," and there was a pause while I thought "Oh dear, she has no idea who I am," and then she said "Jennifer!" just as Paul had when he saw me that morning, "how lovely to hear you." And I said, trying to sound normal "I'm afraid I've got bad news for you, I think you should sit down," and she said "it's Paul isn't it? I knew there was something wrong." And I said, "yes, it is Paul. I don't know if you realized that he was gay, but he is, and I'm afraid he has AIDS."

I tried to get out the explanation in one breath. "He's in the hospital, now, with pneumonia, he's very ill, but if he makes it through this, his doctor says he could maybe live for years. But right now, he's very sick, and I thought you should know."

"I knew there was something," Paul's mother kept saying. "I've been waking up at three every morning, thinking about him..." She was very calm, not hysterical at all; surprisingly, we even laughed a few times. She said she'd often wondered if he were gay, but her husband had always dismissed the idea. Later she said she had known, in her heart of hearts, but hadn't wanted to face it. "Goodness," she said, at one point, "I keep remembering dreadful things I said. Like this friend of his, Nick: Paul told me he was, you know, that way, and wanted him to visit, and I said no, I didn't think I could bear to have him in the house. Oh dear, can you believe I said that? No wonder he never wanted to tell me!"

When I got back to Paul's bedside he was looking drained, his face white, his body rigid. I put my hand on his shoulder and said, "she's okay, she's taken it fine, she says she loves you very much."

Then he cried and cried while I held him, and I felt what must have been twenty years of tension leave his body until he was utterly limp in my arms. I don't think I've ever felt closer to another person in my whole life.

When I called his mother again, this time from Paul's bedside, she was already packing her suitcase. She asked to speak to him; I turned away to give him some privacy, and stared out the window at the sun setting over a wing of the hospital. I heard him say, "oh Mum, you'll never know how much it means to hear you say that," and a few minutes later he was laughing, then apologizing, and I guessed that she was scolding him for telling so many lies for so many years.

It was getting dark when I finally left him to rest. I kissed him good-bye, and he looked up at me and said "it's amazing, suddenly there's nothing left to worry about." And, later, I thought yes, it is amazing. It's amazing how powerful our need for our parents' love and acceptance is. So much so that Paul, staring an incurable disease in the face, was suddenly at peace.

At least for that moment in the hospital, knowing that his mother still loved and accepted him actually meant more to him than whether he lived or died.

EPIPHANY AT ECHO LAKE

When my daughter was eighteen months old, I unaccountably fell into a depression that at times was so oppressive I wished the world would just disappear, or that I could go to sleep and never wake up. The depression had descended, like a storm cloud, after my family and I had come back from a summer vacation in Maine. It worsened as the days grew shorter and the nights longer. I withdrew from the outside world, trapped by a sadness that made me feel scared and lost, and very alone. I retreated from my friends; at times I could barely deal with my children. I spent a lot of time alone, lying on a sofa in my living-room, staring out the window, trying to figure out why I felt so hopeless, why my heart felt leaden when just a few months ago all had been well. I dreamed ugly and disturbing dreams; I became very fearful, jumping at creaks on the stairs or the wind whistling outside. The one thought that kept me going was that in August we would go back to Maine again, and that I would be able once again to swim and stare at the tide coming in and out, and that maybe that would help.

I love Maine. I love the lakes and the trees and the sky, and the swirling, all-enveloping mist. At last August came, and we were back in Acadia, and it was just as beautiful as ever. For the first time in a year I really relaxed; it felt like a wonderful reprieve.

Then, all too soon, the vacation drew to a close; the sun went in, the fog came down, and my heart sank; I thought, that's it, this vacation has just been an interlude, and now it's over. I went with my family for a farewell swim in Echo Lake. It was chilly, about to rain, and I was the only one who really wanted to go. I swam out into the lake and lay on my back, looking up at the sky. A huge cloud of mist was blowing over the trees, obliterating the landscape as it moved. I waited, treading water, wondering what it would feel like to be swallowed up in the mist. A light rain started to fall; surrounded by water, I waited.

And then the mist came, gloriously cool and wet and mystical, and slowly my husband and children on the shore were blotted out, and there was nothing but cool greyness all around me. I was alone in the lake, alone with the mist and the water and the sky. I swam slowly, drinking it in, and as I swam I had a thought, a tiny little thought that bubbled up out of nowhere. I thought, "maybe I could somehow let go of all the pain and sadness, maybe I could just let it flow away with the mist and the water." I turned the thought around and around in my mind as I slowly swam around in the mist.

When I came out of the water, there were children with chattering teeth, and a cold husband, and not enough towels, and it was time to go. I half knew, even as I swam ashore, that something had happened. But it wasn't until weeks later that I realized that what I'd had in the lake was nothing short of an epiphany, a rare and powerful moment of truth. I had let go of a part of my past, of things that could never be undone. In that brief pure moment in the mist and water, something in me had irreversibly changed.

PARTING

It was a dark and stormy night when we left Washington DC to start a new life in Switzerland, myself, my husband Nic, two children, and the baby-on-the-way. I wondered, as we sat grounded for hours on the tarmac while thunder raged all around us, if this was a bad omen. As a child, I remember learning the expression

"partir c'est mourir un peu"—to leave is to die a little"—and I thought of that too, waiting on the runway, wondering what our new lives would hold, mourning what we were about to leave behind us as we sat in storm-bound limbo, not quite gone, definitely not yet arrived.

Then, today, a gift in the form of a letter arrived in our letter box from our friend and former neighbor Richard. "You left on a Wednesday," he writes, "and that night there was a truly fearsome storm, black-scary skies, roaring winds that swirled the treetops and knocked down more than 100 hollow-trunked old trees in Friendship Heights, lightning that blasted houses, torrents of rain. I really did have it in my head that God was angry that you had left, that he was lashing out at all of us for allowing you to leave."

I was very touched by this, not only that our passing did not pass unnoticed, but also that Richard took the time and trouble to write so soon after we had left. And now I'm beginning to realize that partings are really new beginnings, not just new adventures in new lands, but new beginnings also of old relationships. I never wrote to friends who lived in the same town as I; they never wrote to me. We talked on the phone, we shared the minutiae of life, and that I miss.

But now airmail letters are winging their way to and fro across the Atlantic, and suddenly I'm seeing new sides of my friends, finding an unexpectedly caustic wit here and a burst of lyricism there, that somehow went unheeded in ten years of phone calls and dinners and lunches.

And when the skies above Zurich open up, as they did this evening, and thunder crashes and the rains pour down and the church bells toll, I don't think any more of bad omens; I think of Richard's letter, instead, and of friendships, and of distance as a friend, not an enemy.

"HAVE A NICE DAY"

When I used to live in the US, I was regularly descended upon by British friends whose unstated mission, it always transpired, was to establish for themselves exactly what was wrong with the country in general, and with Americans in particular. They all seemed to share one common prejudice: "Americans are so superficial aren't they?" they'd say—overlooking the fact that I, a dual national, count myself as much American as British. "All this over-the-top friendliness. This 'have a nice day' business. Pure hypocrisy!" they'd say. I grew very tired of all this.

Last summer my husband and I and our three small children (all of us dual citizens, ten passports between us) landed back on American soil for the first time in a year and a half; I was curious to see how it would feel. We arrived in Boston after a harrowing flight from Zurich, during which none of us slept, one of us screamed, two of us fought, and one of us, who was quite bored, demanded to visit the bathroom, with parental escort, approximately fifty-nine times. One of us had two Bloody Marys, but even that didn't help.

Eventually, the flight from hell landed. Staggering off the plane with our five pieces of official hand baggage—plus car seat, diaper bag, Brown Bear, Doggy, and four purloined air sickness bags—we proceeded groggily to Customs. "Welcome home!" said the Customs man, handing back our US passports.

Haggard with jet lag, we launched our rental car

into the maelstrom of Boston traffic. Three blocks from the Hyatt Hotel where we were to stay, four-year-old Xanthe said the immortal words "I feel sick." With astonishing speed, given my catatonic state, I grabbed an airline motion-sickness bag, shook it open and flung it under her chin. She sat there glumly holding the bag for another block or two, then said, "I don't feel sick anymore," and gave it back. I leave to your imagination what happened next.

The cleanup operation, conducted with much swearing, used up some four thousand baby wipes and further frayed our tempers. In silence, we drove the remaining half block to the Hyatt. And this is when I discovered that—after just a year and a half away—I have indeed changed.

Our rental car had barely come to a halt when four excessively eager Hyatt employees flung open the doors and launched into a Hearty Hyatt Welcome. "How are we all doin' today?" they bellowed in unison, simultaneously, no doubt, reeling from the stench. "You have a nice day now!" And what did I do? Did I turn to them and smile, thinking, how friendly, how warm, how welcoming... I did not. I winced, grimaced, turned my head away and studiously ignored the lot of them.

As soon as we were safely in our room, I turned to my husband and growled, in worst British fashion, "honestly. How bloody American!"

THE MARMALADE LIE

I thought I had adjusted rather well to our new life here in Switzerland, until I found myself telling a lie: small and inconsequential, but a lie, nevertheless, and one that I never would have told had I still been living in the US. Now I realize how far I still have to go to find my rightful place.

I have moved to a peaceful land of mountains and lakes—where women only recently got the vote. Far behind, like a distant dream, is my former home, a bustling city where sneaker-clad women with bulging briefcases swarm in their power suits to their power jobs in the nation's capital.

We'd been invited to our Swiss friends Lucia and Walter for Sunday lunch, and that morning faced the usual vexed question of what on earth to take with us by way of a gift.

The Swiss are frighteningly generous when they visit—if only for a cup of tea—and are constantly showing up with homemade pies, hand-embroidered bibs for the baby, flowers and herbs from their garden and pots of homemade jam, often all on one occasion.

Sunday visits present a particular problem since the stores are closed, and we were in a state of high fluster—if not outright panic—at the thought of arriving empty-handed until I remembered a lone bakery open on Sundays.

"A pie," said I, with enormous relief, "we'll buy Lucia and Walter a pie." Then I managed to find a spare children's book, and gift-wrapped that for little Andrina and Flurina. As we left, I was still vaguely casting around for more when my eye fell on a pot of marmalade that we had in turn been given the other day by Swiss visitors. I added it to the pile.

Lucia thanked us profusely for the pie and the book. Then she examined the marmalade. "Wonderful!" she said! Pause, while I beamed. "Did you make it yourself?" This is when my heart sank, and this is when, without thinking, I told my lie.

If I were sensible, I would simply have said 'yes,' or perhaps said nothing, looking modestly away. Instead, and I'm not sure quite what possessed me, I said brightly, "oh no, I didn't make it, but my father did!"

Lucia was very surprised. She took the pot of marmalade to Walter and said "Look! Jennifer bought us some marmalade that her father made!" My husband, meanwhile, was looking at me with big eyes.

My Swiss women friends keep trying to teach me to make pies and jams; it's very easy they say, earnestly. Caught between two cultures, I find myself clinging to my non-jam-making identity, while simultaneously flinging out ludicrous fibs in a desperate desire to conform.

An American friend who has lived here for twenty years, assures me this is part of the normal syndrome; "first you'll try and fit in," she said, "then you'll get defiant."

I don't know. I wonder whether I couldn't work on my father to give up on writing and move into large-scale marmalade production.

THE BURGLAR AND THE PINK SHIRT

It was, perhaps, some dim memory of my mother's heroism in Tunisia that came to the fore some fifteen years later, as I stood on the front porch of my parents' house in London and observed yet another a burglar—this one a big, hulking man—rifling through a briefcase in the open doorway of the house opposite. This was the home of our good friends the Kenricks, and I happened to know that the burglar was wasting his time, since what he was ransacking was eight-year-old Diggory Kenrick's school satchel, and all he was likely to find were pens and pencils and rulers and schoolbooks, perhaps the odd half-eaten apple. This, however, made me no less indignant.

I took a deep breath, shouted "What the *@!# do you think you're doing?" and charged across the street. If the burglar was surprised at my sudden arrival, he didn't let on. He looked up from Diggory's briefcase, and stared at me. I was not a little bemused at this point as to how to proceed. In my script, he was supposed to run away, terrified, possibly leaping, like my mother's burglar, through a glass window if there was one handy. Instead, we goggled at each other for a few seconds in mutual disbelief. "I'd better kick him," I thought, in a moment of inspiration. I aimed carefully and kicked out, hard. Unfortunately, I missed.

Clutching the top of his thigh, and looking distinctly irritated, the burglar swore at me, lashed out with his left leg, and sent me sprawling. His aim, I have to say, was a lot better than mine. Then he loped off down the block just as my neighbor Jenny appeared from upstairs, in a bathtowel, and her husband David, fetchingly clad in a pink shirt, arrived back from buying a paper. They were both mystified to find me, gasping, on their doormat. I pointed wildly down the block, and said "burglar!" David set off in pursuit and Jenny, still in her towel, called the police, who arrived quite quickly.

Unfortunately, in my overexcitement I got muddled, and told them the burglar was wearing a pink shirt: an easy mistake to make, but a regrettable one in the circumstances. The police picked up David Kenrick very quickly. He was running along on his own, in the wake of the long-since-disappeared burglar, and it took him some time to convince the police that he was the outraged homeowner, not the miscreant.

Once I got over my embarrassment, I was quite pleased with myself. A woman of action, I thought. Just like my mother. To add to my general cheeriness, I was invited down to Scotland Yard by the police, to look at mug shots to see if I could identify the burglar. Although I had spent several seconds staring at him, standing so close that I could smell his breath, I no longer had the slightest idea what he looked like. Nevertheless, I considered each picture very carefully. Finally, alas, I was forced to concede apologetically to the presiding officer that I couldn't identify the burglar. As I was about to leave, a policeman turned to me and said "you the one that tried to jump the thief?" I nodded modestly. "Big mistake," he said. "Don't do that again.

He could have been armed. Stupid thing to do." I knew he was right, but I argued back anyway. "I had to do something," I objected. The policeman tugged his chin for a moment then produced what still seems to me to be the world's most impractical advice: "What you need to do," he said solemnly, "is to carry a small bag of pepper on you. Throw it into their face. Makes them cry like anything. Just the ticket."

I digested this advice, dubiously, in silence. Then I ran the scene through my mind. "Hang on a second," I'd say to the putative burglar, "I've got something in here for you—"(long pause, while I rummage in my handbag, past keys, tissues, comb, wallet, pens, note-

books, hairbrush, etc.). "Ah!" I'd say finally, with a winning smile, "Here we are! Now if you could just stay right there for a second—."

Something tells me, given my inability to aim straight, that this would never work. In any case, as I approach middle age, I feel I should look for more sedate solutions, such as shrieking for help, or ringing the police.

With any luck, the whole issue has been rendered moot by moving to Switzerland. When we first arrived, I asked our next-door neighbor what crime was like in the area. "Not bad," he said. Then he added, "there was a burglar once, but they caught him."

RUNNING WITH RABBITS

On a recent trip to England, my aunt enthusiastically recommended a book to me: Women Who Run with the Wolves. "It's absolutely marvellous," she said, "you must read it." So I obediently picked up a copy in a bookstore, where I inspected the dust jacket dubiously. I read the first few paragraphs, dipped into the middle, peeked at the end, and put it back on the shelf. Somehow, I doubted the book had much to say to me.

Back at home, sitting at my computer, I hit a mini bout of writer's block, so I decided to go out to the garden to visit our three new rabbits in their run (which is actually large enough to hold a small—if stooped—cocktail party in). A brand-new addition to the family, Flopsy, Mopsy, and Cottontail have rather taken over our lives.

Are there other writers out there, I wondered, lying idly on my tummy in the grass, who retreat to a rabbit run when short on inspiration? There's nothing quite like the pad of tiny paws up and down your back to provoke the muse. (There's also nothing quite like it for provoking the neighbors into staring.)

I've now successfully incorporated Flopsy, Mopsy, and Cottontail into my working day. "I must go and attend to the bunnies," I say loftily to my husband, official-looking pad and pen in hand, leaving him to cope with the children as they hit end-of-day meltdown. Then I go out into the garden and, in Zen-like trance, sieve and rake their trays of litter into aesthetically pleasing patterns, and think great thoughts, and make the odd note on my pad of paper.

Sometimes, I take a book with me; at other times I smuggle in a drink. Occasionally, I just stare into space, being writerly. Recently, during one of these interludes, I remembered the book my aunt recommended, and whiled away a happy minute or two rubbing noses with Cottontail, vainly trying to imagine myself as a woman Running with the Wolves—or even with one wolf.

I concluded, as Cottontail chewed my pen, that there is a need for a whole new movement, and that perhaps I should be the one to found it: Women Who Sit With The Bunnies, I shall call it.

WHEN IN ROME...

When in Rome, do as the Romans do—or at least, try—I thought, doggedly clutching my skis and poles as I skidded my way in too-tight boots through the slush. This was my first—and very likely last—attempt to embrace the Swiss national pastime.

The line for the cable car was several hundred people deep. Kitted out in oversized, borrowed clothes, I had plenty of time to consider how slim and fetching everyone else looked, and to ponder, while fighting claustrophobia, what exactly I looked like. A cross between a Martian and the Michelin man, was my conclusion.

Miraculously, I managed to leap into the moving cable car without impaling myself or anyone else with my ski poles. Far too hot in my woolly hat and gloves, I collapsed in a sweaty heap and shut my eyes as we ascended, since I am afraid of heights. Then I had to wade through miles of snow, banging my skis and poles behind me, before finally catching up with the rest of the group. My feet were freezing, the rest of me boiling, my head itching excruciatingly in my silly hat.

One by one, the other members of the group pushed off, in slow and stately fashion, down the nursery slope. Most needed a gentle shove; the instructor explained that their skis were insufficiently waxed. All I can say is, my skis must have been prepared by someone with a Ph.D. in waxing. I bent my knees and pushed off. Here, reality and my perceptions of it diverge wildly. I felt as if I took off—at approximately 90 m.p.h.—totally out of control, down a sheer precipice. My heart flew out of my chest, and I suffered the worst, most blinding panic attack you could ever imagine. I thought, I'm going to die, and promptly did the only thing I could think of to save myself, which was to sit down.

My husband, who had watched me slide slowly, he assures me, down the marginal incline, was quite surprised. So was the ski instructor, especially when I then said firmly I'd now had enough, and could she please remove my skis at once.

I retired from the fray, shaking and humiliated, and sat on a bench watching the others slithering and sliding, narrowly avoiding being decimated by teenage snowboarders. How on earth can anyone enjoy this? I thought. After lunch—several Diet Cokes, since I had no appetite—I attempted to take the cable car back to the hotel. After half an hour, it dawned on me that while the hotel was downhill, I and my cable car were still heading uphill.

Trapped at 5,000 feet in a tiny, swaying cubicle, desperate for a bathroom as I headed inexorably for the summit and the long, sickening ride back down, I pondered this "when in Rome do as the Romans do" business. Then, in a flash, I saw the light. I mean, the saying isn't when in Switzerland, do as the Swiss do, is it? What do Romans do? They eat pasta, drink wine, stay up late, take long siestas. Come winter, as the slopes of Switzerland grow crowded with kamikaze amateurs, *I* shall be found lolling in a cafe in Rome, happily doing as the Romans do.

THE LADY AND THE TREE

Zurich has the reputation of being a somewhat staid city, peopled by solemn bankers and humorless businessmen, all clockwork precision, and nothing out of place. Certainly no-one ever suggested to me before I moved here that Zurich was a remotely zany place; three recent incidents, however, have made me wonder.

The first occurred on a tram, when my son woke me out of a reverie to point out that the lady two rows ahead of us had a large—and very live—parrot on her shoulder. We watched her get off the tram, shopping bag in hand. The parrot, untethered, perched calmly on her shoulder, observing the burghers of Zurich with an unblinking eye. A few people stared; most, however, acted as if the sight were quite normal.

Incident number two occurred as I was heading to the theatre with my friend Maggie. "My God," she said suddenly "Look! There's a woman walking a tree!" And indeed, across the street from us strode a denim-jacketed woman, trailing a two-foot tree on a leash behind her.

The roots were shedding quite a bit of earth, and passing motorists began to heckle her. "Hey, lady!" shouted one. "Have pity on that poor tree!"

The woman swore roundly at him and carried on, clods of soil flying in her wake. Fascinated, we followed. A man—apparently a waiter—approached, and an altercation ensued.

Maggie and I felt faintly protective toward the woman. OK, so she's nuts, we reasoned, but why shouldn't she take her tree for a walk if she wants? Then she kicked the waiter, and our sympathies shifted fractionally. Limping, he continued to follow her. "It's

my effing Christmas tree!" she shouted, "leave me alone or I'll have you arrested!"

But now a fatal seed of doubt was sown. Even I—a botanical ignoramus—could see this was no fir tree. The leash, however, did look suspiciously like a length of fairy lights. Our play was about to start. Regretfully we abandoned the scene; at last sight, the man and woman were heading in opposite directions, he, triumphantly, with the tree, she with the lights.

After our play ended, we were still intrigued. Retracing our steps, we noticed a telltale trail of earth. Darting up side streets, peering at what turned out to be red herrings in municipal flower beds, we followed the trail back to a sidewalk cafe outside the Hotel Ambassador. There, freshly repotted, and apparently unscathed, stood the little tree. The ground around it was freshly swept. A broken length of fairy lights had been tucked neatly under a flower pot. Calm had been restored.

I mentioned the lady walking her tree and the lady with the parrot to my Swiss friends Christian and Marina, as evidence to support my burgeoning Zurich-is-the-Manhattan-of-Europe theory.

Marina contended that the incidents were isolated anomalies. Christian considered the matter with a lawyerly frown. "Mm. I took a boat across the lake this morning," he said. "On it was a lady with a pram." Marina and I looked at him expectantly. "The pram," said Christian, "was lined with hay."

By now he had our undivided attention. "In the pram," he continued calmly, "was, not a baby, but a rabbit. Apparently the woman was taking her rabbit for a walk. Or, more precisely, for a boat trip."

So now I'm really left wondering about Zurich. One thing I *can* say for sure is that in a decade and a half of living in the States, I never once saw a person walking a parrot, nor a tree, nor a rabbit.

MORNING BLUES

To say that I am not a morning person is an understatement. I struggle through the rituals of washing face, brushing teeth, and ushering children to school, in what can best be described as a state of bad-tempered catatonia. I'd basically given up on myself and mornings until I went to Italy to attend an unusual seminar, held in a huge run-down palace of a hotel, overlooking the Umbrian hills.

I dithered initially, unable to decide between maskmaking, drumming, chi gung, and taking guided blindfold walks around the estate. I wanted to do it all. Meanwhile, I did manage to attend a lecture by an astronomer at Caltech who was studying the far reaches of the universe, and another by an economist, who, it turned out, was also a professional and very accomplished belly dancer. But for me, the highlight of the week was rediscovering the morning, thanks to Irene, a serenely graceful dance teacher in her sixties.

I still don't quite know how I ended up in her 7 a.m. Renaissance Dance class. I resisted fiercely on the first day. Can't possibly, I said to my husband: fear of dancing, fear of groups, fear of people talking to me in the morning, and so on. But by day two, a secondary paranoia had taken hold—fear of missing out. And so, at 6:45 a.m., having been woken by the haunting music of a flute player wandering the darkened corridors, I staggered into my clothes and up the cold stone staircase to the hotel's huge windowed attic.

Shivering, along with some twenty other unconvinced looking beings, we awaited instruction. With Irene's voice ringing out over the music—"Semplice, Semplice, Doppi-o!"—we danced an elegant, courtly dance. And then on to a peasant dance, which soon became entirely chaotic, people whirling accidentally from wrong partner to wrong partner, feet treading on feet, a roomful of people suddenly laughing, where ten minutes before they had stood huddled and yawning. I whirled, danced, lost the rhythm and found it, twirled with strangers, grinned at my husband—imagine his shock—and was, in short, happy, in a way that I have not been in the morning for thirty years or more.

And now I am back in Switzerland, facing overcast skies, lost homework, and fractious children. I wish I could say I am magically transformed; to my family, I'm afraid, I am still less than charming in the morning. And yet, inside, I am a little changed. To feel joy, to feel different, to feel free of the confines of being what you think you are, if only fleetingly, is indeed a small transformation.

I shall send a post card to Irene, I think. "I'm not exactly dancing in the mornings," I shall write, "but once in a while, I do remember, and I smile. For which I thank you."

DISPOSAL OF CADAVERS

I figured there'd be one or two adjustments to make when I moved from the US to Switzerland. What amazes me is that three years later, I'm still grappling with the intricacies of the garbage system.

Rule number one is that you can only put your garbage bags out at a specified spot on the curb, on Monday and Thursday mornings. Swiss friends warned us that if we disobeyed, we risked being reported to the police. Rule number two is that each trash bag must be adorned with a special label, which costs the equivalent of two dollars, to support the system. The stickers are burglar-proof, carefully perforated for once-only use, designed to foil wicked souls who might try to peel one off a neighbor's bag.

No sooner had we mastered the art of stickering our trash without ourselves ripping the label to shreds, than we received our first copy of the local Annual Garbage Calendar—a riveting treatise which outlining the exact procedures and dates, given a year ahead, for disposal of, amongst other things: cardboard, batteries, glass, paper, electronic items, large and small, and garden refuse, not including roots or weeds. I read on, fascinated, and discovered a garbage category I'd never even considered. "Hey, Nic," I called to my husband, who was in the garden, dutifully sorting roots and weeds. "You'll never believe this. There's a section on the proper disposal of cadavers." Until we'd figured out the German, this was cause for some speculation. If an aged relative, say, expired on our premises, would we have to deep-freeze them until the appropriate month? How many stickers should we put on? Should we measure by volume, as per the instructions for large electrical items, or by weight? We'd only been here a few months when I woke up one morning and realized with horror that I'd failed to put the cardboard out by eight a.m., as instructed, and it was now ten past. Frantic, still in pajamas, I shot down to the basement and set about feverishly stomping on scores of boxes, a legacy from our move which we'd been tripping over for ages. In a frenzy I flattened them, flung string around them, and dragged them onto the sidewalk. At noon I checked. Still there. And nothing outside anyone else's house. I called the Garbage Inspectorate's number, and grovelled. "I'm afraid I missed the deadline," I said in broken German, "and there are one hundred and three cardboard boxes outside my house and it's three months before the next pickup!" They transferred me here, there, and everywhere. Eventually, they put me through directly to the driver of the pickup truck. I told him my story, expecting him to be gruff and unsympathetic, and was pleasantly surprised when he engaged me in conversation. "Where were you in the States?" he asked. It turned out he'd been to Washington DC and had liked it. "Tell you what," he said, "on my way home for lunch I'll drive by your house." At exactly eleven-fifty, a large truck roared up. I dashed out just as he was pulling away, in time to catch a big smile and a wave. As I waved back, I thought, hey, I can live with this system.

OF LICE AND FLEAS

My agent Theresa hasn't known me long, so I was both pleased and determined to impress her when she took a detour from the Frankfurt Book Fair to see me. A woman of many virtues, she is, among other things, exceedingly well-groomed. It was, therefore, unfortunate that five minutes after she'd arrived a teacher called to say my daughter Xanthe had been scratching her head and was suspected of having lice. Theresa, as yet childless, had trouble suppressing her horror. "Impossible!" she said firmly. "Your children are so charming, so clean!" Charming and clean they may be, but it soon transpired all three of them had lice.

As we walked together to the drugstore, Theresa updated me on the Frankfurt Book Fair and expounded on the merits of small versus large publishing houses, while I tried to appear cool, calm, and collected. Then, as I shampooed, showered, and generally disinfected the children, Theresa, perched on the edge of the bathtub, outlined her strategy for my new novel. Later that evening, she fled, with ill-disguised relief, back to the sanctity of her home in Geneva.

The lice, however, stayed. My theory is that the local breed has grown resistant to Swiss shampoos; our pediatrician hotly denies it. (In fact, he denies they're Swiss lice to start with, but that's another story.) During the next six months, the lice pretended to retreat only to reappear again weeks later. We used eight different shampoos, four kinds of combs, and three anti-lice sprays. I personally logged sixteen back-breaking hours of hand-to-louse combat, sitting with successive children under a spotlight, searching for and removing individual eggs, hair by hair, with the help of tweezers and a magnifying glass.

Countless conversations with doctors and pharmacists produced contradictory advice. In desperation, I called an American lice hotline, which revealed that a product one doctor had just recommended can be fatal to children. A kind friend in London took to the Internet on our behalf, and faxed three pages of suggestions, including that one should daub the hair thoroughly with a tubful of margarine, then wrap it in cling film and leave it overnight. (This we did not try.)

As I approached a state of near hysteria, my husband, a chemist, decided the culprit must be the children's soft toys, which we had soft-heartedly failed to boil properly lest we destroy them.

He proceeded to haul home a huge metal vat of liquid nitrogen from his lab, and, in the kitchen, amid billowing clouds of vapor, we quick-froze Xanthe's little dog Silky, Dylan's Brown Bear, and Lucy's beloved Dolly. Finally the lice—probably bored, rather than defeated—departed.

My main worry now is how to undo the impression made on Theresa. I did not help matters the other day when I told her, over the phone, that we'd been away and had thoroughly enjoyed visiting a flea market. I bit my tongue, too late. After what felt like an interminable pause, Theresa said thoughtfully, "A *flea* market. How nice. And did you come away with anything?"

EGG MONEY

When I was nine years old, I made my mother what I thought was a perfectly sensible proposition: "If I walk to school instead of taking the bus, can I keep the bus fare?" My mother looked at me appalled, with one of those looks that speaks reams. Then she said: "If you follow that sort of logic, you'll start saying you don't want your boiled egg at breakfast, and can you have the money for it?" In vain did I deny I would ever do such a thing. The subject was closed.

Many years later, I relayed this story to my husband. Somewhat disloyally—I feel—he took my mother's side, and proceeded to coin the expression "egg money" to embrace my peculiar financial idiosyncrasies. He has a hard time, for example, accepting my habit of hiding money in books. When our cleaning lady was sick for several months, I squirreled away the amount that we would have paid her in a volume entitled, "The Letters of Henry Root." One day, I unveiled the stash to my husband. He was incredulous that I had been hiding money from him. "That's not the point at all! I was hiding it just as much from myself," I protested. "But you knew where it was!" he said, with irrefutable logic. Eventually, he calmed down, sighed, and said, "It's Egg Money all over again, isn't it?"

What he sees as eccentricity—or perhaps mental abnormality—is, in my view, a perfectly laudable capacity for lateral thinking. One should be creative with money, all the more so if one doesn't have enough of it. I still remember the winter—not so very long ago—when we lived mostly on lentils, and kept the heating turned off in the house to save money. To keep warm, I wore my hat and coat indoors, which was occasionally embarrassing when I absentmindedly answered the door thus attired.

Now, for the first time ever, I find myself comfortably off—which is novel, and in many ways great. But for a person dedicated to the concept of creative financing it's also a bit dampening. Where's the challenge?

Friends of ours visiting from England remarked that they wished they could afford a computer for their son; given their teachers' salaries, they said, and the state of their finances, they'd have to win the lottery first.

Aha! thought I: a challenge! With some excitement, I propounded my egg-money ideas. "Honestly," I said airily, "it's all matter of looking at things in the right way!" Our friends were not convinced.

Meanwhile, I was facing another problem. My children were supposed to be going off to a summer camp, to give me some much-needed writing time. Annoyingly, they were balking at the idea.

"You had such fun, last year!" I kept saying. "No we didn't, we hated it" they kept countering. Then inspiration struck.

I phoned our teacher-friends in England and asked if they would come over during their summer vacation and run a joint two-week camp for our children and theirs. They agreed enthusiastically, before I'd even got to the part about how we could then reroute the saved summer-camp money into a brand-new Computer Fund.

And now the computer is long since bought and installed. Our friend's son, at age 14, is so expert on it, some of his computer tips are about to be published, and our two families are in constant communication in Cyberspace, adding a whole new dimension to our friendship.

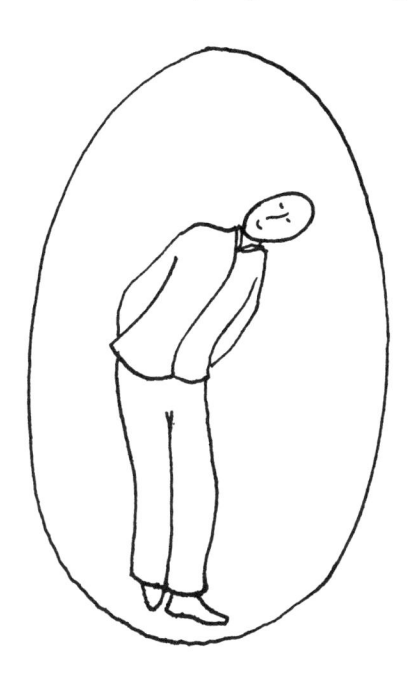

And I, at last, feel vindicated: If my egg-money theory were a person, I think it could safely stand up at this point and take a bow!

FREE TO GO

My friend Paul—already endowed with more warmth, wit, and generosity than the average bear—has always been one of the funniest people I know. Even as AIDS and dementia were ravaging his body and mind, his sense of humor remained intact. He remarked once that his hospital roommate's arm was looking disturbingly like a loaf of French bread. I said I wondered why. "Because I'm hungry, of course!" he said, quick as a wink.

I asked him later whether he thought he was confused or had dementia, and he said, in a flash of lucidity, "well, medically speaking, it's the same thing. One just sounds worse than the other."

We had many surreal—and sweet—conversations. "So what have you been up to?" I asked him one morning, knowing the answer full well: lying in bed, watching his IV drip, listening to his roommate cough hackingly, and throw up. "I've been travelling," he said. I enquired where to. He thought for a moment, then said, "The Great Barrier Reef." I accused him of being a jet-setter, and he laughed. Then he spoke of snorkeling, and the beauty of the fish, and the coral, and I, too, in turn, was transported.

He was extraordinarily stoic as the disease took its course; his favorite words were "I'll be fine," his main worry always how his mother, alone in the world, would cope.

Near the end I flew over to say good-bye. Lying on

his bed together, in the dark, we spoke again of journeys. He said he worried about finding his passport, was anxious he hadn't packed everything. Above all, he was still worrying about his mother. I said she'd be fine, that it was time to think of himself. I said it was a big journey, but he was probably as prepared for it as he could be. Staring out the window at the night sky he said, "it would be all right at 84, but it's a bit odd at 48." In fact, he was just 40, but I knew what he meant.

In my last phone call to him he could barely speak. I asked his mother to hold the receiver for him, and I sang, rather quaveringly, two songs I used to comfort my children with when they were small. His mother said he struggled to speak, but couldn't.

At the very end, when he could no longer be comfortable at home, he went into a hospice. He had, at this point, almost none of his faculties left, and was in pain. He was given morphine, and went into a coma. Still he clung on, against all odds. I knew he was still worrying about his mother. I told her maybe he needed her permission to die. She seemed doubtful.

In the end, though, alone in the room with him, with no way of knowing if he could even hear her, let alone understand, she told him that she loved him, that he had struggled long enough. She told him she would miss him, but that she would be all right. She told him he should feel free to go. Then she left the room.

No-one will ever know what, if anything, was going through his mind then. But within an hour of his mother telling him that he was free to go, Paul finally, very quietly, died.

FLASHBACKS

I've thought about death quite a bit over the years. My father had a serious heart attack, which he recovered from, but which forced me for the first time to face his—and my—mortality, and the same year that my friend Paul died of AIDS, another friend of mine, Ann, a vibrant anthropologist in her sixties, went upstairs and lay down for a nap from which she never woke up. I have often wondered what Ann and Paul felt when their final moment came.

When I was eleven, I had a brush with death which, in retrospect at least, I find a curiously comforting experience. I was living an uneventful life in Brussels at the time, attending the local French Lycée.

The morning-I-nearly-died started out much like any other, with me swinging my legs out of bed, and reaching to turn on my bedside light. The lamp had, unbeknownst to me, developed a lethal wiring defect.

Suddenly I was in the grip of something extraordinarily powerful, which shook me violently and wouldn't let me go. I was stuck like a limpet to the metal lamp, shaking uncontrollably as the electric current—all 220 volts of it—surged through my arm, down my body, and, via my foot and the radiator, into the ground.

I remember thinking with enormous clarity and calm "I'm going to die." Right after that, I thought "I don't want to die." I was trying to scream, but no sound was coming out. Strangely, I didn't feel scared at all.

I had a bizarre and distinctly unscientific—but, as it

turned out, lifesaving—notion that if you touched wood, you couldn't be electrocuted. The nearest piece of wood was the headboard of my bed, and I found that although my right side was paralyzed, I could still move my left arm.

I reached behind me, and stretched to touch the headboard. (Later, I realized this movement had dislodged my foot from the radiator, and thus from the ground.) As my hand touched the wood, the current stopped flowing, my clenched right hand unclenched, the lamp fell to the floor with a crash, and I was still eleven, and still alive.

That, at least, is what happened on the outside. Inside, my mind had been racing simultaneously down several tracks. First came the matter-of-fact realization that I was going to die, and the overwhelmingly clear conviction that I didn't want to. Then I had the inevitable "dear God—" conversation that even nonbelievers embark on in emergencies.

After that came flashbacks, to a gentle time when I walked as a child in England with my grandmother across a little wooden bridge, and knelt to feel the water below, and she said "mind your sleeve, dear, it'll get wet," and I felt the cold water creeping up the arm of my navy blue cardigan, the one with pale blue pearl-like buttons, and she just smiled at me.

And I thought, even as the electric current was rushing through me, Wow! You really do get flashbacks when you're about to die! And now I'll never get to tell anyone!

And I distinctly remember feeling put out.

I often think if I had died then, how people would have thought it a terrible way for a child to die, and that's where I take comfort: Even as I fought dying, I felt a great, enormous, empowering, all-encompassing sense of calm. Although I'm inexpressibly glad I didn't die, I'm also very grateful that I nearly did.

I suffer when I think of my family dying, or my friends. But I feel lucky to be largely unafraid of my own death.

I think I know what it's like, and I think it's going to be all right.

FROM GUNS TO BRUISES

When I lived in Washington DC, I complained from time to time about life in the nation's capital. It was mostly the violence in the city that troubled me, which seemed with every passing year to come closer to home. One day, however, the complaints stopped: Push had come to shove, and we were off, to Switzerland, where a whole new life awaited us.

Mundane routines came under new scrutiny as I weighed up our present and future lives. At 8:30 one sunny morning, I left the house to take my children to one of their last days of American school. Before I drove off, I undid the cumbersome steel device that locked my steering wheel in place, which I had bought when both my car and my neighbor's were stolen from right outside our houses; I locked both doors, silently remembering Pam Basu, who worked with my husband and was killed September 8, 1992, in a carjacking.

Then I set off, enjoying the sunshine and the chirping of the birds. The Janney Elementary School gates weren't open yet, though dozens of children were gathered. Thinking of random snipers—such as the one who had been recently prowling the Adams Morgan neighborhood—I stayed in the car, watching, until the school doors opened and my son was safely inside.

On the way to my daughter's day-care, I stopped at a four-way stop sign at a quiet intersection, at the same time as another car. It didn't move, so I pulled out. The driver of the other car shot out in front of me, flicked his middle finger, shouted an obscenity, and screeched off in a cloud of dust. All this before breakfast.

At that point, the scales were definitely tipped in favor of Switzerland. Then my son Dylan asked if they would have an "International Day" to celebrate all the foreign kids at his new Swiss school, and I had to say no, I didn't think so, and I felt a pang. The Swiss are known for a certain protective insularity, and I wondered how he and we would fare as foreigners in a small, perhaps close-minded country.

I remembered how a Russian boy, Dimitri, had joined my son's American kindergarten class midyear, and how Mrs. Williams, the teacher, took such pains to make his assimilation a class project. Dylan would come home saying proudly "guess what! Dimitri knows three words now: "hi, playground, and bathroom!"

Not surprisingly, things are very different in Switzerland. During the preschool years, while many American kids are busy being "socialized" and learning their ABCs, Swiss children are mostly at home with their mothers, thus arriving at "big school" relatively unprepared. Perhaps because of this, they are a lot rougher with each other than their American counterparts. At recess, there is typically no teacher present, and some quite aggressive fights can break out, which are expected to be resolved without adult intervention.

Schoolchildren walk to and from school alone, several times a day, since they all come home for lunch. (Even pint-sized five-year-olds can be seen tromping off unaccompanied, hovering, slightly bemused, at pedestrian crossings.) This journey, though short, can be an ordeal if a bully pounces and if there is no adult in sight. For the first six months of first grade, our son—who then spoke no Swiss German—was routinely attacked on the "Schulweg," as the route home is known, arriving back home bruised and ashen-faced.

Swiss friends sympathized, but were unsurprised. Many of them recalled similar episodes from their own youth. "It's a rite of passage," they said, shrugging. "You must teach your son to fight back." So, after years of instilling concepts such as "use your words," we changed tack.

Our son took up judo. He also learned the language, at which point his problems ceased. But other kids—by no means all foreign—still suffer: the overweight ones, the ones who can't run very fast, the slow ones, the different ones.

I am puzzled. We left a city where bullets fly and kill every day, where schools have security guards and metal detectors, in a country known for going to war. We also left behind classrooms where children use words, not fists, and where respect and non-prejudice are taught.

We moved to a well-organized, beautiful country, internationally known for its non-aggressive stand, a country which has not been to war in 500 years. But in this peaceful, otherwise delightful land, children fighting—even seriously hurting—each other is by and large accepted, condoned as part and parcel of growing up.

Did the wires get crossed somehow along the line?

THERAPY AND QUICHE

I have seen a number of therapists over the years—in both England and America—and I reckon I have pretty well grasped the basics of the system. While the patient, cocooned in total privacy, airs for exactly fifty minutes their innermost thoughts, the therapist plays a benevolent—if slightly bizarre—role, answering questions with questions and resolutely sidestepping any remotely personal inquiries such as "so where are you going on vacation?" and "was that you I saw in Safeway, buying cat food, and asparagus?"

I assumed, therefore, when I set off for my first appointment with a Swiss therapist, that the system would be basically the same in this well-ordered, sometimes conventional country.

I let myself into the basement of his house—via the open back door, as instructed—and wandered, unescorted, past piles of old shoes and bits of sporting equipment.

I peered at a few semi-framed pictures, propped up against a wall, and took inventory of the laundry hanging on a line. Then I paused before the door of what I deduced must be the consulting room, removed my shoes, and padded in, in my stockinged feet, to await the good doctor.

I had a few minutes to inspect his bookshelves before he arrived, slightly flustered, shook my hand, and sat on the floor, a few feet away from the cushions where I had ensconced myself. There was no clock in the room, no windows, no pictures, no desk: nothing really, except some books, a lamp, and a carpet. I found it curiously restful.

The room was quite silent, apart from the sound of the doctor's stomach loudly rumbling. He acknowledged this with a self-deprecating smile and admitted, when I daringly probed, to being hungry.

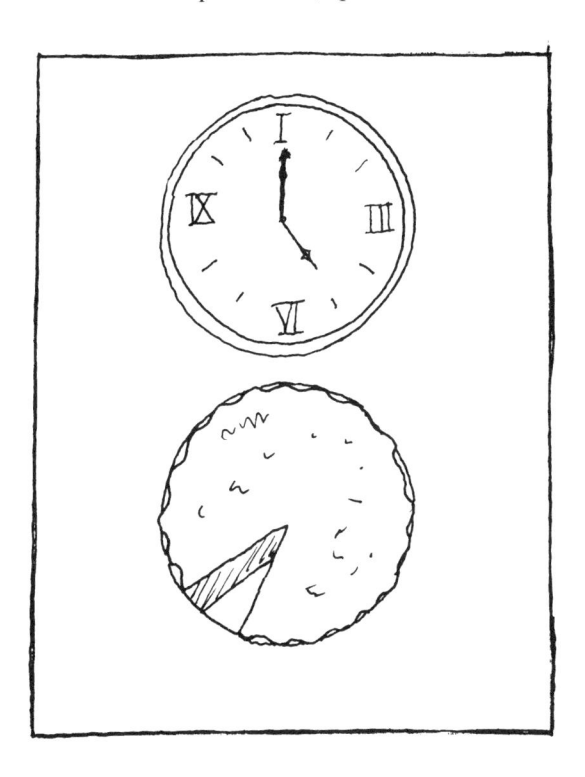

After forty minutes or so, just as I was mid-flow, a knock came at the door. "An emergency!" I thought, with a rush of adrenaline. It had to be serious for someone to break the sanctity of the therapist's room. The doctor leaped to his feet, opened the door a crack, and proceeded to conduct a quiet, very intense-sounding conversation with someone out in the hall.

"What's happened?" I thought, straining to overhear, though he was speaking in Swiss German, which is a fairly impenetrable dialect for me, even at normal volume.

I was busy conjuring up scenarios of suicidal patients and wondering whether to retreat and cede my time-slot to whomever it was, when he closed the door and resumed his seat on the floor. He looked very serious. "I am so sorry," he said. "My son is having a problem."

I raised my eyebrows, simultaneously concerned and questioning. "He is making a quiche," explained the doctor, "and he didn't know what temperature to cook it at. It is the first quiche he has made."

I suppressed the urge to laugh. The doctor was looking morose. "I think he has burned it," he added, and his stomach let out a particularly loud, gurgling rumble.

At this point I could no longer control myself, and I burst out laughing. He looked at me quizzically, then chuckled too. After that, he told me the best way, in his opinion, to make a quiche, and we overshot the fifty-minute mark by far.

Unorthodox as it was, I have to say it was far and away one of the best—and most memorable—therapy sessions I've ever had.

A PIECE OF ADVICE

The Swiss are remarkably fond of dispensing advice. They will tell you, at the drop of a hat (and in the nicest possible way) what you are doing wrong with your compost pile, how to rearrange your furniture so you are no longer in any danger of sitting in a draught, and even—a peculiar obsession, this—how to prevent weasels from climbing undetected into your car's engine at night and chewing up the rubber tubes within. "Let me give you a piece of advice," they say, at the beginning of every other sentence.

Although I noticed when we first moved here that everybody and his brother seemed to know better than we how to do things, I did not fully grasp the pervasiveness of this national trait until my first visit to our family doctor.

I told him that I was feeling low and suffering from winter blues. "Well, you should go away, of course! Escape the winter!" he said. He moved briskly into the role of travel agent, recommending a trip to Luxor, Egypt, where he had just had a pleasant vacation with his wife; he was so enthusiastic, I half expected him to produce a stack of holiday snaps out of the pocket of his white coat.

When I said Luxor was likely to be unaffordable for our family of five, he was undeterred. "Take to the mountains, then, to find the sun," he declaimed, "you can do it in a day," and went so far as to recommend which mountain and the best route there.

Unfortunately, we failed to discuss the crucial matter of where to eat on this particular mountain. When I described, on my next visit to him, the overpriced, unfriendly cafe at which we had dined, he threw up his hands in horror (a quintessentially Swiss gesture).

"If only you had walked a little further!" he said. "Just ten more minutes. There is a marvelous restaurant there, very good value, serving the most wonderful venison!"

I have learned to expect advice at any time, and from any quarter. "Just where are you planning to plant that?" a neighbor will say, dubiously eyeing me, my trowel and a small tree.

Cornered, I point to the spot I had in mind. "Heavens! It'll never grow there," they say. "You should get it professionally planted. By someone who knows what they're doing." The depressing thing is, more often than not they are quite right.

So I live, and try to learn. Every day, I myself become a little more Swiss. (My son caught me sweeping the front doorstep the other day and shot me a distinctly ironic look, as if to say "and who do you think you're kidding?")

The other day, a new English-speaking person moved into the neighborhood, and I went around immediately to introduce myself. "Will you be sending your kids to Swiss school?" I enquired. The neighbor nodded.

"Ah well," said I, and wouldn't you know it, before I could stop myself, the words "Let me give you a piece of advice" popped right out of my mouth.

The following pieces have aired on National Public Radio's All Things Considered:

Contrary Old Lady

A Dizzying Selection of Parts

Chasing Pimples

Thomas the Tank Engine

Home Again!

My Friend Paul

Intervention

Have a Nice Day!

The Marmalade Lie

When in Rome...

Disposal of Cadavers

Therapy and Quiche

Egg Money

A Piece of Advice

ABOUT THE ARTIST

Ann Arnold was born in San Francisco in 1952. When not painting still life (in oil on wood), she illustrates children's books, including Alice Waters' Fanny at Chez Panisse (1992), Ranjitsinhji's 9000 Elephants Visit Serendipity Books (1996) and Sara London's Firehorse Max (1997). She lives in Berkeley, California.

DEAR READER...

If you have enjoyed this book, please help it find its way into more living rooms, onto more people's bedside tables, into more bathrooms, briefcases, or backpacks.

Stop Smelling My Rose! is being advertised largely by word of mouth, by kind people like yourself, as well as via my home page on the world-wide web, where I welcome visitors.

> **http://www.jenniferdavidson.com**

If you visit, and I hope you will, you will find some photos and pictures which relate to these stories, a more detailed biography, as well as an ongoing column of book reviews.

Overleaf is information about ordering.
Please tear it out or photocopy it for anyone you know who might enjoy this book.

With many thanks,

Jennifer Davidson

ORDER FORM

To order copies of
Stop Smelling My Rose!
please send a check, made out to
"Redgrove Press," to:

in North America: Redgrove Press,
PO Box 9075, Berkeley CA 94709
$11.95 plus $3.50 p&p
(California residents, please add sales tax)

in the UK: Redgrove Press,
45 Lamont Road, Chelsea, London SW10 OHU
£7.95 plus £2.00 p&p

in Switzerland: Redgrove Press,
Neuhausstrasse 20, CH-8702 Zollikon
19.50 Swiss Francs plus 5 Francs p&p

Please send Stop Smelling My Rose! to:

_____

_____

_____

I enclose a check for   (incl. p&p)